■ SCHOLASTIC

C000180722

create and display

Art and Culture

Full of exciting activities and displays for the whole curriculum

Ages 5-11
for all primary years

Claire Tinker

SCHOLASTIC

Book End, Range Road, Witney, Oxfordshire, OX29 OYD
www.scholastic.co.uk

© 2011, Scholastic Ltd

1 2 3 4 5 6 7 8 9   0 1 2 3 4 5 6 7 8 9

British Library Cataloguing-in-Publication Data
A catalogue record for this book is available from the
British Library.

ISBN 978-1407-12527-5
Printed by Bell & Bain Ltd, Glasgow

Text © 2011 Claire Tinker

Claire Tinker hereby asserts her moral rights to be
identified as the author of this work in accordance
with the Copyright, Designs and Patents Act 1988.

All rights reserved. This book is sold subject to the
condition that it shall not, by way of trade or otherwise,
be lent, hired out or otherwise circulated without the
publisher's prior consent in any form of binding or cover
other than that in which it is published and without a
similar condition, including this condition, being imposed
upon the subsequent purchaser.

No part of this publication may be reproduced, stored in
a retrieval system, or transmitted, in any form or by any
means, electronic, mechanical, photocopying, recording
or otherwise, other than for the purposes described in
the lessons in this book, without the prior permission of
the publisher. This book remains in copyright, although
permission is granted to copy pages where indicated
for classroom distribution and use only in the school
which has purchased the book, or by the teacher who
has purchased the book, and in accordance with the CLA
licensing agreement. Photocopying permission is given
only for purchasers and not for borrowers of books
from any lending service.

Due to the nature of the web we cannot guarantee the
content or links of any site mentioned. We strongly
recommend that teachers check websites before using
them in the classroom.

Commissioning Editor
Paul Naish

Development Editor
Emily Jefferson

Editor
Tracy Kewley

Series Designer Andrea Lewis

Cover Design Sarah Garbett

Designer Sonja Bagley

Photography
Alan Sill

Acknowledgements

The author and publisher would like to thank
the children at Dore Junior School, Sheffield, for
their enthusiasm and wonderful artwork that is
featured in the displays in this book.

The author would particularly like to thank the
staff and headteacher Sue Hopkinson for their
huge support and generous help.

Finally Claire Tinker would like to thank her ever
supportive family and friends for their enthusiastic
interest and wonderful encouragement during the
writing of this book.

Images:

Page 6, Tutankhamun's golden funeral mask ©
photos.com/Getty Images; page 8, Pyramids at Giza
© Holger Mette/istockphoto; page 12, Part of the
Elgin Marbles © markrhiggins/shutterstock; page
13, Ancient Greek silver tetradrachm coin of coiled
serpents issued 128-123BC © Kenneth V. Pilon/
shutterstock; page 13, Greek silver coin with owl
motif © Paul Picone/shutterstock; page 16, Ancient
Roman silver tetradrachm coin of Vespasian who
ruled 69-79AD © Kenneth V. Pilon/shutterstock;
page 21, Part of the Bayeux Tapestry: English King
Harold II on visit to Normandy, 1064 © photos.com/
Getty Images; page 24, *Summer* 1573 by Giuseppe
Arcimboldo © The Gallery Collection/Corbis; page
30, Landscape painting with children fishing near a
lock, 1823, JMW Turner, (1775-1851) © Image Asset
Management Ltd./SuperStock; page 35, Untitled
massive sculpture in a plaza in downtown Chicago
by Picasso © Thomas Barrat/shutterstock; page
36, Firebird by Niki de Saint Phalle in the Stravinsky
Fountain adjacent to the Centre George Pompidou,
Paris © Bruce Martin/Alamy; page 42, *The Great
Wave off Kanagawa* by Katsushika Hokusai (1760
- 1849), woodcut, circa 1831© INTERFOTO/Alamy;
page 50, Cornhusk doll craft © Manook/
istockphoto; page 52, Aztec Turquoise Mosaic of
Double Headed Serpent from Mexico 15th-16th
century, British Museum, London, England © Steve
Vidler/SuperStock; page 57, 19th Century willow
pattern plate © Science and Society/SuperStock;
page 67, Masai wedding necklace © Fabrizio Cianella/
istockphoto; page 70, Blue sky over Moai at Rano
Raraku, Easter Island, Chile © Grafissimo/
istockphoto

All other images © Scholastic Ltd.

Contents

Introduction

Create and display: Art and Culture is an introduction to the history of art, organised into two main categories: western art and art from different cultures. The first section of the book is intended as a loosely chronological overview of some of the main periods in western art. Written histories of western art often begin with the paintings of ancient Egypt from around 5,000 years ago. This was followed by a period called ancient Classical art which began in Greece more than 2,500 years ago. By 150BCE, the Romans, although based in Italy, had conquered most of Europe. They were great admirers of Greek culture and made many copies of Greek sculptures and techniques. The Romans are famous for their architecture and introduced many new building techniques.

The first 500 years after the collapse of the Roman Empire was a time of great unrest and fighting, often known as the Dark Ages. During this early medieval period, the monasteries played an important role in keeping art and literacy alive. They were principal centres of learning and culture, spreading the Christian message and producing illuminated manuscripts of religious texts. During this period, the Angles, Saxons and Jutes moved into Britain and, in the late 8th century, the Vikings came from Norway, Sweden and Denmark. They all brought distinctive art forms of their own.

In the 15th and 16th centuries there was a great cultural revolution. Renaissance means 'rebirth' and it is a term that describes a renewed interest in the classical art and culture of ancient Greece and Rome. It was a great cultural movement, a period of revival but also one of renewal and growth. It influenced not only art but all aspects of life from architecture to science, literature, philosophy and astronomy.

The Renaissance started in Italy, and the city of Florence was at the heart of the movement. One of the great features of this period was an entirely new way of painting using oil-based paint which enabled artists to work more slowly and create ever more realistic paintings. Around 1413CE, the architect Filippo Brunelleschi developed the rules of perspective. This was an important breakthrough in the history of art.

The Renaissance period lasted approximately 200 years but by the 17th century, a new style of painting called Baroque was emerging. It was an impressive dramatic style. It was followed in the 18th century by Rococo art, sometimes referred to as Late Baroque. It is an ornamental, decorative and fun style and some people dismissed it as frivolous. This period only lasted for around 40 years. In the late 18th century there were many wars and uprisings. The revolutions in America and France challenged old ideas and governments, and gave people a sense of power to demand a better way of life.

The 19th century heralded a new era of exciting scientific theories and discoveries, which became known as the Industrial Revolution. This period of art history is sometimes known as the era of revolutions and many new art movements and styles emerged, with artists reflecting upon and responding to the changes around them. The movements and related sub-movements are too numerous to list but the three covered in this book are Romanticism, Impressionism and the Arts and Crafts movement.

The art of the 20th century was characterised by enormous richness and complexities. It was a time of great change as artists challenged established assumptions and ideas. Artists began to experiment with new styles and techniques, and individuals with similar aims and ideas often joined together to form a movement. This century saw the birth of abstract art movements that present challenges to the viewer to respond to the concepts and ideology within it.

The second section of the book covers some of the world's huge diversity of artistic styles and techniques. Studying arts and crafts from different cultures provides a fascinating starting point for further investigation, discussion and exploration of the countries and cultures featured in a cross-curricular format. This book is by no means a comprehensive or definitive coverage of either western art or art from different cultures. Its aim has been to attempt to further children's understanding of the artistic world around them and inspire cross-curricular creativity and enjoyment.

Claire Tinker, March 2011

Ancient Egypt

Egypt is an ancient desert country situated in north-east Africa. In ancient times, the river Nile, which runs south to north through the country, flooded every year, making the surrounding land very fertile. The civilisation of ancient Egypt lasted for more than 3000 years, starting in about 3100BCE and ending with the Roman occupation in 30BCE. Pharaohs were the kings or queens and the most powerful people in ancient Egypt. One of the most famous pharaohs today is Tutankhamun (1341–1323BCE). He became pharaoh when he was a boy and reigned for about ten years from approximately 1333–1323BCE. When he was alive Tutankhamun would not have been a particularly significant pharaoh but he is very well known today because his tomb was discovered in 1922 by Howard Carter and his team of British archaeologists. The tomb was discovered in the Valley of the Kings on the west bank of the Nile and many treasures were found inside, the most famous of which was the solid gold funerary mask of Tutankhamun.

Tutankhamun Screen Prints

Resources

- Pictures of Tutankhamun's funeral mask
- Cartridge paper
- Coloured paper in blue and/or gold
- Silk-screen and squeegee
- Poster paint in blue and or/gold

Approach

1 Tell the children the story of Tutankhamun and draw a timeline on the board to show when he lived. Show the children pictures of Tutankhamun's golden funeral mask. Explain that it is 54cm high and made from gold, glass and semi-precious stones.

2 Prepare a stencil by drawing a simplified version of the mask on a piece of cartridge paper.

3 Cut out the parts that are to be a different colour from your chosen coloured paper.

4 Place the stencil on the coloured paper and lower the screen on top. Use a squeegee to pull the paint evenly from the top of the screen to the bottom. This may take a couple of pulls.

5 Remove the screen. The paper stencil should stick to the screen leaving the cut-out areas printed.

6 Repeat this process with the other colour combination.

Wire Symbols

The ancient Egyptians used signs and symbols called hieroglyphs to communicate information. The word *hieroglyph* literally means 'sacred carving'. There were more than 700 different hieroglyphs. Some of these were pictures, others represented sounds. The Rosetta Stone, which was carved in 196BCE, helped historians to decipher hieroglyphic writing. It was discovered in 1799 and is covered in writing in three different scripts: hieroglyphic, demotic and ancient Greek. Historians understood the Greek writing and realised that if all three texts told the same story, they would be able to work out the meaning of some of the hieroglyphs.

Resources

- Ancient Egyptian hieroglyphs
- Examples of modern-day symbols
- Cartridge paper
- Thin wire
- Beads

Approach

1 Discuss the term *symbol*. Explain that symbols are a way of communicating information quickly and simply. Provide examples of both modern and ancient Egyptian symbols. Discuss their messages. Show the children pictures of hieroglyphs and talk about their meanings and how we are able to interpret them.
2 Prepare ideas by drawing a symbol or hieroglyph onto plain paper.
3 Demonstrate how to bend the wire into the shape of hieroglyphs.
4 Add beads to embellish the designs.

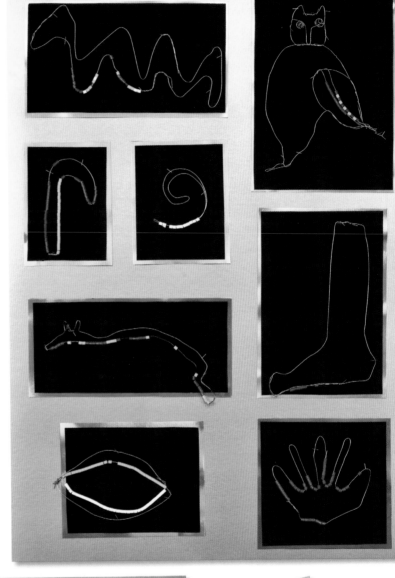

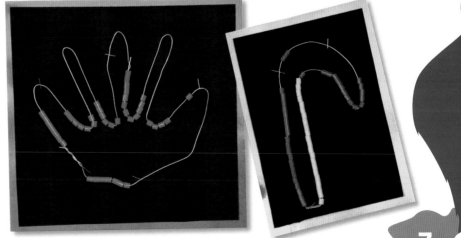

Papyrus Pyramid

Pyramids are religious monuments and the tombs of ancient Egyptian kings and queens. The Egyptians believed that if a pharaoh's body was mummified after death, the pharaoh would live forever. Pyramids were built next to the Nile and were positioned to align with sacred star constellations. Gods and goddesses were very important to the ancient Egyptians and many Egyptian tombs had paintings of different gods on the walls. Egyptologists think that the shape of a pyramid was intended to help the pharaoh climb to heaven, and that the sloping sides represented the rays of the sun god, Ra.

Resources

- Triangular pieces of papyrus
- Felt pens or gold pens
- Pictures of ancient Egyptian gods
- Cardboard

Approach

1 Tell the children that papyrus is an early form of paper made in ancient Egypt. Explain that it is made from the pith of the papyrus plant which is cut into thin strips. The strips are placed on a hard surface with subsequent strips placed at right angles on top.
2 Encourage the children to study the papyrus to see the results of this process.
3 Explain that gods and goddesses were very important to the ancient Egyptians and they were often shown with a human body and the head of an animal or bird. Research some Egyptian gods and goddesses, such as Amun, Horus, Isis and Ra.
4 Give the children a triangular piece of papyrus to decorate with a picture of an Egyptian god.
5 Place all the triangles together around a giant pyramid.

create and display: Art and Culture

Book of the Dead Frieze

The *Book of the Dead* scrolls were written to help ancient Egyptians travel through the netherworld to the afterlife. They were a collection of spells written in hieroglyphs on papyrus. They were rolled up and put inside a hollow statue then buried in tombs with the dead. Some spells allowed the dead person to turn into different animals, making it easier to navigate the landscape of the netherworld and reach the afterlife.

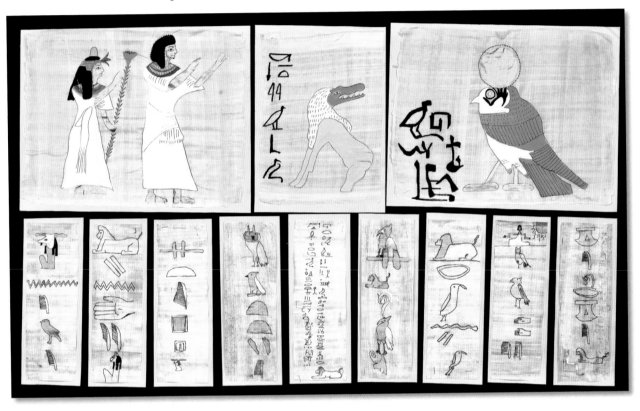

Resources

- Rectangular pieces of papyrus
- Felt pens or paint in gold and white
- An example of the *Book of the Dead of Hunefer* (or an image from the internet)
- A copy of the Egyptian hieroglyphic alphabet

Approach

1 Explain that the ancient Egyptians believed that the *Book of the Dead* would give them special powers and keep them safe on the journey through the netherworld to the afterlife. The scrolls contained spells in hieroglyphs and beautiful illustrations. Point out that hieroglyphs are written in vertical lines and read from top to bottom.
2 Give the children a piece of paper to copy a transformation spell or to write out their own name, using a copy of the hieroglyphic alphabet to help them.
3 Explain that the *Book of the Dead of Hunefer* was 5.5 metres long and 39cm tall. On a sheet of papyrus ask each child to design their own part of an ancient Egyptian Book of the Dead.
4 Put all the pieces together as a frieze.

Cross-curricular Links

- **Maths** – Discuss how the pyramids were made. The Great Pyramid was an outstanding feat of engineering and contains over 2.3 million blocks of stone. Find out more facts about pyramids. Make paper nets and construct your own pyramids.
- **Geography** – Each year from June to September the Nile flooded with melting snow from the Ethiopian highlands. The floodwater fertilized the soil for the harvests. Research why the Nile had such influence on ancient Egyptian life, and why the Nile doesn't flood today.

Ancient Greece

Ancient Greek art covers a huge time span and is divided into four main periods: Geometric (900–700BCE) Archaic (700–480BCE), Classical (480–323BCE) and Hellenistic (323–31BCE). Greece has one of the longest cultural traditions in the western world and the earliest evidence of Greek art comes from a period of time long before the Geometric period and can be traced back to about 3000BCE and the Minoan civilisation, named after the legendary King Minos. Greek myths are traditional stories that were created in an attempt to understand the environment, as an explanation for difficult concepts or to provide wise lessons for how to live a good life. They were often about gods and goddesses, heroes, heroines and monsters and one of the most famous Greek myths was about King Minos and the Minotaur. Images of Greek myths were often used to decorate coins, pottery and buildings.

Minotaur Theatre Costume Head

Resources

- Withy canes
- Masking tape
- PVA glue
- Sponges
- Tissue paper
- Felt and other collage materials

Approach

1 Soak the withy canes in water for an hour or so to make them more pliable.
2 Demonstrate how to bend the canes to make a frame for a Minotaur's head. Attach the canes together with masking tape.
3 Make a mixture of PVA glue and water in a bowl and use a sponge to carefully cover a sheet of tissue paper with the glue.
4 Drape the tissue paper over the withy frame and cover with a layer of the PVA mixture so that the tissue paper dries hard.
5 Decorate with felt and collage materials.
6 The head can be used to perform the story of 'Theseus and the Minotaur'.

Geometric Vases

Although art from the Greek Classical period is probably the best known, art from the other three periods is equally distinctive. The Geometric period lasted from about 900BCE to about 700BCE. The name of this period describes the geometric decoration used, particularly on pottery. Geometric vases were surrounded by continuous bands of circles, wavy lines, zigzags, nets and triangles.

Resources

- Pictures of Classical Greek and Geometric vases
- Outlines or stencils of Greek vases in different shapes
- Cartridge paper
- Black pens
- Black and clay-coloured paints
- Brushes
- Balloons
- Scrap paper
- Papier-mâché paste

Approach

1 Make a timeline of the different Greek periods. Explain that the Classical period was the most famous and that a lot of the Greek art shown in books is from this period. Display pictures of Classical Greek vases showing figures and characteristic scenes from mythology. Note how the decorations were painted in black and how the background was left the orangey-red colour of the clay. Explain that vases from the Geometric period were slightly different. Discuss the meaning of *geometric*. Show examples of vases from this period and discuss similarities and differences.

2 Provide examples or stencils of different shaped vases and ask the children to sketch out geometric patterns on a piece of paper and transfer their designs onto the vase.

3 Make a 3D vase from papier-mâchéd balloons and decorate with geometric designs.

Parthenon Frieze

The Parthenon was a temple dedicated to the Greek goddess Athena. It was built nearly 2,500 years ago between 447–438BCE on top of a hill called the Acropolis. Inside the Parthenon was a statue of the goddess Athena, heavily adorned in gold, and outside there was a frieze decorating the four walls. The frieze is about 160m long, one metre high and carved from marble. Over the centuries a large part of the Parthenon was destroyed and by 1800 only about half of the frieze remained. Part of the frieze was brought to Britain in 1803 by Thomas Bruce, Seventh Earl of Elgin (1766–1841) and purchased by the British Museum in 1816. There has been much debate about where the marbles should be kept. You could arrange a visit to the British Museum to view the 'Elgin Marbles'.

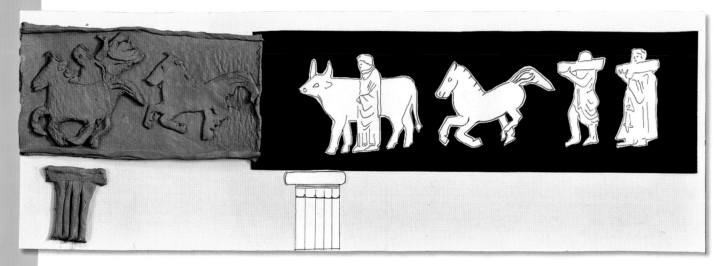

Resources

- Pictures of the Parthenon frieze
- Cartridge paper and pencils
- Self-hardening clay
- Clay tools
- PVA glue

Approach

1 Show the children pictures of the Parthenon and explain the history of the building.
2 Give the children pictures of the Parthenon frieze and explain where it was originally located. Divide the frieze into sections and allocate sections to groups of children. Discuss how the frieze would have looked when new and encourage the children

to draw in the missing parts in their section.
3 Roll out a slab of clay and ask the children to copy their part of the frieze onto it.
4 Allow the clay to dry then brush with diluted PVA. Place all the parts together as a frieze.

Greek Coins

In ancient Greece each city minted its own coins. They were handmade, often out of silver, and each state was represented by a different picture. An owl was the emblem of Athens, one of the most powerful cities in ancient Greece. Athenians put a picture of an owl on their coins.

Resources

- Pictures of ancient Greek coins
- Heavy tinfoil or lightweight embossing foil
- Pencils
- Cardboard

Approach

1 Show the children pictures of ancient Greek coins.
2 Sketch out some designs on a sheet of cartridge paper.
3 Cover a piece of cardboard with foil and transfer the design onto the foil using a blunt pencil.
4 Ask the children to design and create a coin depicting something important for their own town or city.
5 Research the Greek alphabet and include a suitable ancient inscription.

Cross-curricular Links

- **Literacy** – In Greek mythology, the Minotaur was locked up in a labyrinth at the vast palace of Knossos on the island of Crete. Rewrite the story as a cartoon strip of sequences and design a maze for the Minotaur to live in. Alternatively, tell the story of Heracles. Identify the twelve labours. Ask the children to sketch out their ideas of how they imagine the different tasks and different monsters would look. Transfer ideas into a cartoon strip. Children could also research the Greek alphabet.
- **Numeracy** – Draw shapes with Greek-derived names, for example, pentagon, hexagon. Explore the children's knowledge of words and examples they may know which are also Greek-derived, e.g *pentathlon, octopus!*

The Romans

Rome is the capital city of Italy and modern historians believe it was founded in the year 625BCE. As Rome expanded from a small kingdom into a republic, then an empire it exported its language, art and culture across the Mediterranean and beyond. One of the best known art forms of ancient Rome is the mosaic. Mosaics are pictures made from small fragments of tile, glass or stone called tesserae. (An individual piece is called a tessera.) Roman mosaics depicted scenes of animals, birds, people and gods, and they decorated walls and floors.

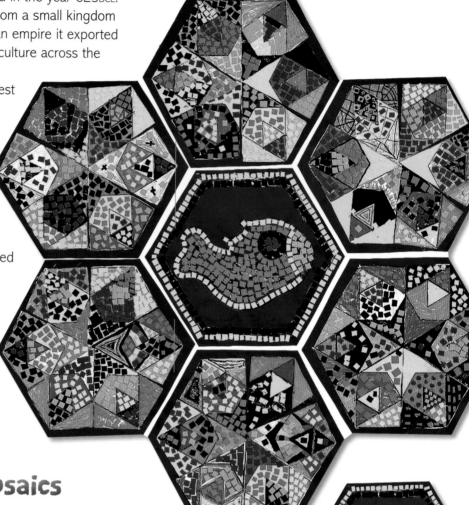

Roman Mosaics

Resources

- Pictures of Roman mosaics
- Large sheets of coloured cardboard
- Mosaic pieces in paper, foam, felt or any safe hard fragments of material
- Glue and spreaders

Approach

1 Show the children pictures of Roman mosaics (for example, the black and white floor mosaic of sea creatures from the Roman city of Volubilis in North Africa) and discuss the patterns, shapes and colours that were used. In Roman times, several artists would work on one mosaic, so children could be encouraged to work in pairs to design a mosaic.

2 Draw the outline of the design onto a large sheet of card.
3 Stick pieces of mosaic material onto the design, leaving a small space between each piece.
4 Experiment with different materials and discuss which gives the best effect. Tell the children that Roman tesserae were first made from natural materials like marble and limestone but later on small pieces of glazed ceramic and coloured glass were also used.

Roman Sculpture

The word sculpture comes from the Latin word *sculpere* which means 'to carve' or 'to chisel'. It is the art of creating three-dimensional shapes or pictures. Although Roman sculpture was heavily influenced by Greek art, it had many distinctive features. Whereas the Greeks were famous for their idealistic portrayal of people, the Romans were known for their realism and showing a person's characteristics. A lot of the sculptures commissioned were of rich and powerful people. They were made from marble which is crystallized limestone rock. Statues of emperors were copied and put up all over the empire to remind people of Rome's power.

Resources

- A picture of the marble bust of Hadrian, found at his villa in Tivoli
- Polystyrene heads
- Mod-Roc
- Photos of marble busts of various emperors, such as Julius Caeser
- Paints and brushes

Approach

1 Tell the children that Hadrian was a Roman emperor who ruled from 117 to 138CE. Ask them if they have heard of Hadrian and talk about his influence in Britain (Hadrian's Wall).

Show the children a picture of the marble bust of Hadrian that was found at his villa in Tivoli in Italy. Discuss how the portraits were more realistic than Greek ones and ask the children what this bust communicates about the Emperor Hadrian.

2 Research the different Roman emperors and place them on a timeline. Collect pictures of sculptures of them and ask the children to make detailed drawings of them.

3 Use Mod-Roc to sculpt the features of the emperors on top of the polystyrene heads.

4 Paint the busts in 'marble-coloured' paint.

5 Put the sculptures together to create a three-dimensional timeline.

Roman Coins

The earliest Roman coins featured gods such as Mercury, Janus and Apollo. Julius Caesar was the first emperor to place a portrait of himself on a coin. From then on Roman coins always featured the reigning emperor and historians believed they used them as a way of communicating their achievements and spreading information.

Resources

- Pictures of Roman coins
- Self-hardening clay and clay tools
- Cartridge paper
- Silver and gold paints

Approach

1 As a class, research the life of Julius Caesar. He was born on 13 July 100BCE and died on 15 March 44BCE, a date known in the Roman calendar as 'the ides of March'. He was the most famous of all Roman generals and many coins were made with his portrait, including one that depicted the event of his assassination. Search the internet or look in books for some examples.

2 Using the research information about his life, invite the children to design a new coin for Julius Caesar. They should think about the message it would portray and how the emperor would have wanted to be viewed by the public.

3 Ask the children to transfer their designs onto clay, using the implements to carve or indent the coin.

4 When the coins are dry, the children can paint them in silver or gold. Tell them that a silver coin was called a *denarius* and a gold coin an *aureus*.

Roman Architecture

The ancient Romans are famous for their architecture. Although they looked to the Greeks for models, they had many new ideas of their own. They used arches in their designs which not only made the construction stronger but also allowed them to create decorative and triumphal gateways that were used for victory processions. They also used arches to build domes, which were made up of a number of arches rotated in a circle. The most famous example of this technique is in the Pantheon, a temple built by Emperor Hadrian to honour all gods. It was built in Rome between 117 and 125CE and still has the world's largest unreinforced concrete dome. The tallest building in ancient Rome was the Colosseum. It was built of bricks and concrete, an ancient Roman invention, and had seating capacity for approximately 50,000 people. In the arches were statues of gods and heroes. The Colosseum was a venue for gladiatorial and animal fights.

Resources

- Pictures of Roman architecture
- Tracing paper
- View finders
- Potatoes and cutting tools
- Poster paints

Approach

1 Show the children pictures of Roman architecture. Use the information above to talk about the features and inventions of ancient Roman architecture.
2 Give the children view finders and encourage them to highlight a particular feature of interest on a building, for example, an arch. Ask them to draw it on squared paper or use tracing paper in the same way as modern architects.
3 The children can then transfer their shape outlines onto a section of cut potato. Adult help will be needed to carve out the shape.
4 Let the children print shapes using thick poster paint.

Cross-curricular Links

- **Literacy** – The word 'arena' comes from the Latin for 'sand'. Research other Latin words in our vocabulary.
- **Maths** – Create maths challenges based on Roman numerals:
  I = 1; V = 5; X = 10;
  L = 50; C = 100;
  D = 500; M = 1000.

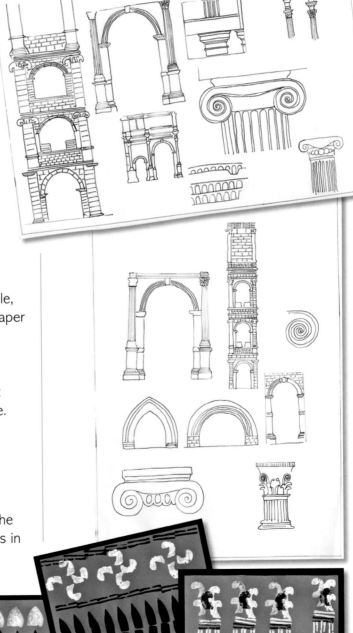

The Medieval Period

Medieval art is the art from the Middle Ages from about 476CE –15th century CE, a period of approximately 1000 years, which is sometimes sub divided into Early, High and Late Middle Ages. It follows the collapse of the Roman Empire around 410CE when the Roman armies were recalled from Britain and other areas, and is generally agreed to end with the advent of the Rennaissance which began in Florence, Italy. After the Romans left, monks in the Christian Church played a vital role in keeping literacy and art alive. All books during this period were handwritten on parchment or vellum, which is specially treated animal skin. The manuscripts were exquisitely decorated with the initial letter at the beginning enlarged and beautifully decorated. The manuscripts were coloured in ink, coloured pigments and 'illuminated' with gold leaf. They were stitched together, attached to a wooden or leather spine and took hundreds of hours to complete.

Illuminated Manuscripts

Resources

- Pictures of illuminated manuscripts
- Cartridge paper
- Ink pens
- Coloured inks
- Gold paint
- Medieval music (optional)

Approach

1 Show the children examples of illuminated manuscripts. One of the best examples is the *Book of Kells,* which was probably produced by Celtic monks in a monastery on the island of Iona. It is thought that, after a Viking raid, it was moved to Kells in Ireland for safekeeping. Draw the children's attention to the initials or letters at the beginning of the texts and the incredible intricate patterns and designs.

2 Give the children a piece of cartridge paper and ask them to design their own decorated letter. When the monks were copying out the writing they had to follow the rules of no heating, no lighting and no talking. Try to create a quiet monastic atmosphere and, if possible, play medieval music for the 'scribes' to listen to as they work on their designs.

Stained-Glass Windows

In the Middle Ages, religion dominated daily life and many churches and cathedrals were built. As most people in medieval times couldn't read or write, pictures were used to teach people about the Christian religion. Churches were filled with paintings, sculptures and stained-glass windows, all depicting religious scenes of biblical history. The stained-glass windows were designed like mosaics with small pieces of coloured glass held in place by lead frames, and they filtered light in many beautiful colours.

Resources

- Pictures of stained-glass rose windows
- Paper and pencils
- Compasses and protractors
- Round sheets of acetate
- Glass paints and outliners

Approach

1 Explain that during the early Middle Ages churches were built in the Romanesque style with stone columns, round arches and vaulted ceilings. Later on they were larger and built in the Gothic style, with pointed arches and bigger windows. The Gothic style of architecture provided more opportunities for large stained-glass windows.

2 Show the children pictures of stained glass windows.
3 The children should then design a pattern on their window using the examples for inspiration.
4 Ask the children to place a sheet of acetate over their paper and trace over their shape with glass outliners. When the outlines are dry, they can fill them in with glass paints.
5 Draw a picture of a religious scene for the centrepiece and display as one large window.

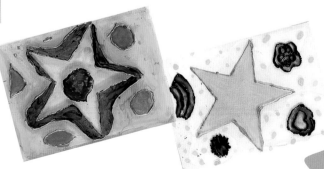

19

Sutton Hoo Treasures

In 1939 archaeologists in Britain excavated the remains of an Anglo-Saxon ship burial, possibly the grave of Redwald, king of the East Angles, who died around 625CE. The ship had rotted away but some of the treasures buried in it had survived, including silver ornaments, jewellery and armour.

Resources

- Pictures of the Sutton Hoo treasures
- Cardboard
- Scissors
- Silver or gold embossing foil
- Collage materials, including sequins
- Glue and spreaders
- Cardboard masks
- A suitable version of the 'Beowulf' story, such as *Beowulf* by Kevin Crossley-Holland (OUP 1999)

Approach

1 Tell the children the story of the discovery of the Sutton Hoo treasures in 1939. Explain that archaeologists are like detectives and discuss the significance of the finds at this site.

2 Show pictures of the treasures found in the ship, including the shield and helmet. The shield is jewelled and has emblems of an eagle and a six-winged dragon crafted on it. Explain that dragons were very common in Anglo-Saxon art and can be found decorating jewellery and on the prows of ships.

3 Give the children a piece of round cardboard and ask them to design their own shield. Invite them to decorate it using embossing foil and collage materials.

4 Look again at the pictures of the helmet and discuss how it would have looked when it was originally made. Make a 3D picture of the helmet using a cardboard mask and recreate how it might have looked originally with embossing foil and sequins.

5 Read the children the story of Beowulf which is an Anglo-Saxon poem about a monster called Grendel. Discuss its possible links to the Sutton Hoo burial ground.

The Bayeux Tapestry

The Bayeux Tapestry tells the story of the Norman Conquest of England. In 1066 the Saxon King, Edward the Confessor (1003–1066CE) died without an heir. William Duke of Normandy (1028–1087CE), claimed that he had been promised the throne. When Harold Godwinson (1022–1066CE), a Saxon lord, was crowned King, William invaded England. The two armies fought a battle at Hastings. According to legend, King Harold was killed by an arrow in his eye. William became king and was crowned in Westminster Abbey on Christmas Day 1066, ending Saxon rule in England. The Bayeux Tapestry is not actually a tapestry but a series of embroidered panels, approximately 50cm high and 70m long.

Resources

- A picture of the Bayeux Tapestry scene that depicts Harold's death
- Collage materials and glue
- Coloured threads and needles
- Large piece of fabric   ● Felt

Approach

1 Tell the children the story of the Battle of Hastings and put some major events on a timeline to show when it took place. Explain that the Bayeux Tapestry tells the story of the Battle of Hastings from the Norman perspective, and discuss how the Saxons may

have interpreted the battle differently. Explain that, although tapestries were common in medieval times, this is not a true woven tapestry but sewn embroidery.

2 Show the children a picture of the final tapestry scene, which shows Harold being killed. Interpret the Latin writing above the picture HIC HAROLD REX INTERFECTUS EST, meaning 'Harold has been killed'.

3 Ask the children to create their own picture of the final scene using felt and other collage materials. They could use embroidery to enhance the tapestry.

Cross-curricular Links

- **History** – In 1086, William the Conqueror ordered the Domesday Book to be compiled. It was a complete inventory of Britain, the first national census. Research the Domesday Book and discuss how historians use it to find out what life was like in the 11th century. You could also research laws in the Middle Ages, including King John and the Magna Carta.
- **Literacy** – Animate a scene from the Bayeux Tapestry by making models out of clay. Write scripts to accompany the film.

The Renaissance

Renaissance means 'rebirth' and is a term that applies to a period of art spanning more than two centuries. It is sub-divided into the Early and High Renaissance periods. The Early period started around 1400 in Florence, Italy, where there was a renewed interest in classical art and ideas from ancient Greece and Rome. The High Renaissance is generally thought to cover the years between 1495 and 1520. One of the most important figures of the Renaissance was Leonardo da Vinci (1452–1519). He was a man of many skills: a painter, engineer, scientist, sculptor, mathematician and inventor. He was incredibly curious about the world around him and studied the human body, astronomy and botany. He left behind a wealth of notebooks crammed with detailed drawings and inventions.

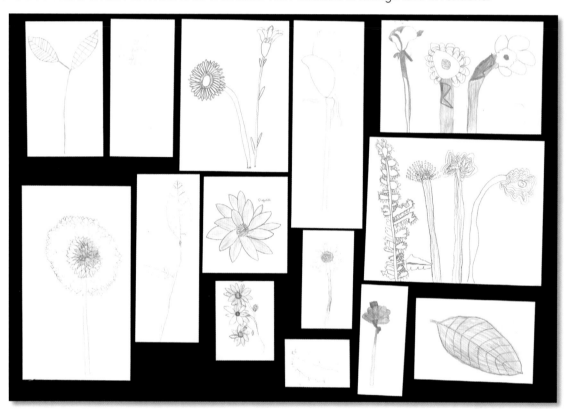

Leonardo Drawings

Resources

- Copies of Leonardo's drawings of flowers and plants
- Cartridge paper
- Mixed drawing media, for example, pencils, charcoal, pen and ink

Approach

1 Talk to the children about the life and work of Leonard da Vinci. During his lifetime he made countless studies of plants, architecture, people and scenes from nature. He recorded his sketches in notebooks which were often accompanied by thoughts and notes written in back-to-front mirror writing.

2 Provide a variety of media and encourage the children to experiment and make as many different types of mark as they can.

3 Give out examples of Leonardo's studies of flowers and explain that the challenge is to produce an accurate representation of the flower or plant in front of them. Allow time to observe the composition carefully.

4 Group together several observational drawings of the same plant, but created using different media, in your display.

Tudor Portraits

In Tudor times only the rich and powerful had their portraits painted. They were often commissioned to show off their power, wealth or status and convey a message. One of the most famous Tudor portrait painters was Hans Holbein the Younger (1497–1543). He was born in Germany and was the son of a painter. He travelled to England in 1526 and by 1535 he was court painter to Henry VIII. In the reign of Queen Elizabeth I, Belgian painter Marcus Gheeraerts the Younger (1561/62–1636) was an artist of the Tudor court. The medium for Tudor portraits was oil paint on wooden panels in the earlier period and on canvas during the reign of Elizabeth I.

Resources

- Small canvasses (one per child)
- Thick poster paint and brushes
- Cardboard for the frames
- Collage materials
- Glue
- Pictures of Tudor portraits

Approach

1 Research the different kings and queens of the Tudor period and, as a class, make a royal family tree.
2 Discuss why Tudor monarchs commissioned paintings of themselves (to show off their power and status).
3 Show the children pictures of Tudor portraits and encourage them to look carefully by asking questions about the compositions. For example: *Do you think the King/Queen really looked like this?* (Tudor portraits tended to flatter the sitter.) *Why do you think this? What are they wearing? What message is the King/Queen trying to portray? What clues are there in the use of objects and symbols in the painting?*
4 Ask the children to choose a Tudor monarch, then to research their life and compose a portrait of them. Research Tudor symbols in paintings and encourage the children to choose appropriate ones to convey a message in their own compositions. For example, Queen Elizabeth I was shown standing on a map of England to show domination over her kingdom.

Arcimboldo Portrait

Giuseppe Arcimboldo (1527–1593) was an Italian painter best known for his clever portraits of heads made entirely out of fruit and vegetables. He was born in Milan, the son of a painter, and grew up in the time of the High Renaissance. He began his career by designing stained-glass windows for Milan cathedral but, in 1562, he left Italy to become the portraitist to Ferdinand I (1503–1564) at the Habsburg imperial court in Vienna. He stayed there for 25 years and served as an artist to three generations of emperors and kings. Under the patronage of Emperor Maximillian II (1527–1576) Arcimboldo painted the series of paintings entitled *Four Seasons*. Arcimboldo is remembered for his distinctive style of painting that was very different from the other painters of his day.

Resources

- Pictures of Arcimboldo's *Four Seasons*
- Pictures of flowers and fruit
- Cartridge paper
- Collage materials
- Glue and scissors

Approach

1 Show the children pictures of Arcimboldo's *Four Seasons* series of paintings. Discuss which fruits or flowers are used to make up each season. Which do the children like the best? Why? Explain that the paintings were created more than 400 years ago but that this style was not typical of the time. The paintings do not just represent the four seasons but have a deeper meaning about the ageing process of humans.

2 Take photographs of flowers and fruit, or cut them out of magazines. Ask the children to choose a season to create a collage in the style of Arcimboldo.

Tudor Decorative Carvings

The Tudors created the distinctive 'black and white' effect style of houses. They were made from a wooden framework of beams, and the spaces between the blackened timbers were filled with wattle and daub. Wattle is made from small woven sticks and daub is a mixture of wet clay and sand which was smeared over the wattle. The internal walls were adorned with decorative oak panelling which helped to keep out the drafts. Patterns were carved onto the panels, and popular motifs were the Tudor Rose and the 'linen fold', a type of decoration that looks like folded linen.

Resources

- Pieces of balsa wood
- Clay tools
- Lollipop sticks or matchsticks
- Corrugated cardboard
- Scissors and glue
- Dark brown paints and brushes

Approach

1 Research information about Tudor homes. Discuss the style of architecture and internal decoration.
2 Create balsa wood panelling by pressing a blunt clay tool into the soft wood to make carving patterns. Use lollipop sticks or matchsticks to develop the pattern.
3 Make cardboard panelling by rolling corrugated card. You can create interesting patterns by adding folds as you roll.
4 Make matchstick printing blocks by drawing a geometric 'black and white' architectural design onto cardboard. Cover with matchsticks. Allow to dry and print with black paint onto white paper.

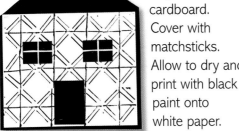

Cross-curricular Links

- **Geography** – Great discoveries took place during the Renaissance period. Research the travels of Christopher Columbus and Sir Francis Drake. Plot their voyages of discovery on a world map.
- **Science** – Look at a copy of *The Arnolfini Marriage* by Jan van Eyck (1395–1441). Draw the children's attention to the mirror in the centre of the composition. Explain that it is a convex mirror (curving outwards) which expands the viewer's field of vision and gives a slightly distorted view. (Flat mirrors were very expensive in van Eyck's day.) Provide the children with small plastic convex mirrors to study their reflection. Ask what images they can see beyond their own reflection and describe how it has been distorted. Give the children a circular piece of paper and ask them to draw the image from the mirror in as much detail as possible.

The Baroque Period

Baroque is the name given to the style of art and architecture that emerged across Europe in the late 16th to the early 18th century. Baroque architecture was an exaggerated style designed to impress. Baroque artists wanted to show life how it really was and painted scenes of ordinary people and everyday life. Still life was also very popular and often contained hidden messages, symbols and meanings. Two of the most famous Baroque artists were Caravaggio (1571–1610) and Jan Vermeer (1632–1675).

Baroque Still Life

Resources

- Cartridge paper
- Crayons, paints and brushes
- Collection of fruit

Approach

1 Explain that the term 'still life' is used to describe a picture of commonplace items, natural or manmade, in an artificial setting.

2 Show examples of Baroque still-life paintings (such as Caravaggio's *Basket of Fruit* or *Still Life with Fruit*). Look at the composition of the arrangements, for example, the triangular compositions. Study the light effects and how it affects the mood of the painting.

3 Demonstrate how to arrange a composition of fruit or flowers and encourage careful observation of the composition.

4 Ask each child to study and draw one fruit of their choice. Encourage the children to sketch their fruit in pencil first, then use paints and crayons to add colour.

5 Display all the different fruits together. You could add some insects and discuss the symbolism of putting insects in paintings.

Rococo-Inspired Paper Sculpture

Rococo art, sometimes considered a frivolous indulgent art of the aristocracy, succeeded the Baroque style. The name Rococo comes from *rocaille* which in French means 'shells', and Rococo is characterised by its uses of curving scroll-like shapes similar to those represented in shells. Furniture, ornaments and architecture all contained a prolific use of curving, elaborate, ornamental and irregular designs often based on natural forms.

Resources

- Pictures of Rococo sculpture and architecture
- Paper plates
- Cartridge paper
- Art straws
- Glue
- Scissors

Approach

1 Show the children some pictures of Rococo sculpture and architecture. Discuss the flowing, curving style.
2 Paper sculpture is an easily accessible medium for creating Rococo-style scrolls and decorative forms. Provide the children with a paper plate and paper. Demonstrate how to curl paper around a pencil to create curls.
3 Allow the children to experiment with different forms of paper sculpture and transfer their ideas into individual flower patterns.
4 Display the flowers in a 3D papier-mâché vase.

Cross-curricular Links

- **Science** – It is thought that some Baroque artists used a camera obscura to help them turn 3D scenes into 2D pictures more accurately. Investigate how a camera obscura works and discuss how it could be used as a drawing tool for artists in the 17th century. Use a projector to project an image upside down onto a wall. Trace the upside down image onto a sheet of paper in the way the Baroque artists would do. Paint the picture that is reflected and compare to the original scene.

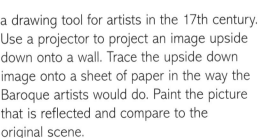

The Revolution Era

The Pre-Raphaelites were a group of British art students who admired the values of medieval painters who pre-dated Raphael (1483–1520). (Pre-Raphaelite means 'before the time of Raphael'.) Pre-Raphaelite art often depicted scenes from books and placed strong emphasis on direct observational painting. William Morris (1834–1896) was an English Pre-Raphaelite. He was a leading member of the Arts and Crafts movement which rejected the mass production of machine-made goods and aimed to re-establish the values of traditional craftsmanship. He is best known for his pattern design for which he drew his inspiration from nature.

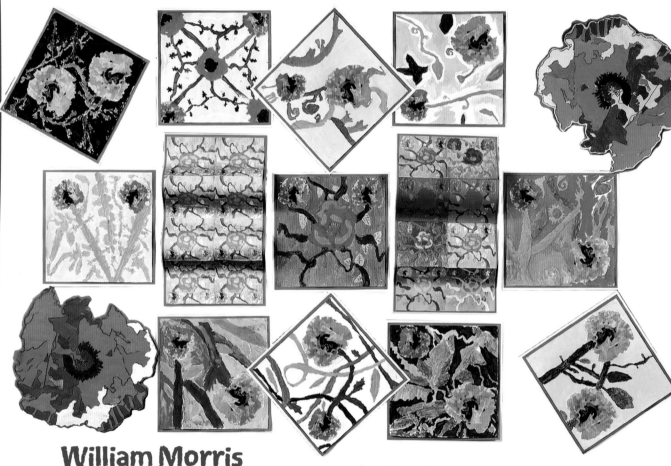

William Morris

Resources

- Pictures of William Morris designs
- Viewfinders
- Cartridge paper
- Paint and brushes

Approach

1 Show the children pictures of designs by William Morris. Discuss his use of colour and the inspiration for his work.
2 Provide viewfinders and ask the children to highlight a particular area to enlarge and copy.
3 Invite them to copy and then paint the pattern. You could photocopy the designs then join them together to make a roll of wallpaper.
4 The children could also use ICT packages to create repeating William Morris-style designs. They could digitally change the colour schemes for the designs and make up a wallpaper design catalogue for the class.

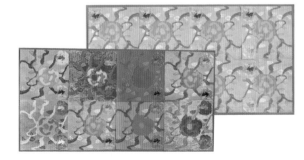

Charles Rennie Mackintosh

Charles Rennie Mackintosh (1868–1928) was a man of many talents, an architect, artist and innovative designer of furniture, metalwork, textiles and glass. He helped to pioneer the period of decorative arts called the Arts and Crafts movement. He was born in Glasgow, where most of his surviving work is kept.

Resources

- Pictures of Mackintosh stencil designs
- Pieces of white cotton fabric
- Black and gold paint and brushes
- Pieces of sticky-backed plastic
- Scissors

Approach

1. Explain to the children the background to the Arts and Crafts movement and show pictures of Charles Rennie Mackintosh's stencil designs.
2. Sketch out a simple pattern and transfer it onto the paper backing of the sticky-backed plastic. Demonstrate how to cut out the stencil. Place the stencil onto the fabric and paint. Carefully peel off the design and repeat the process.
3. Let the children have a go at creating their own stencil designs.
4. Display the designs with some more stencils printed onto paper to create a roll of Charles Rennie Mackintosh wallpaper.

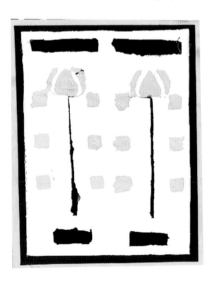

Turner Skyscapes

During the late 18th century there were many wars and uprisings. The revolutions in America and France challenged old ideas and governments, and gave ordinary people a sense of power to demand a better way of life. Alongside the political revolutions, the 19th century heralded a new era of advancement which became known as the Industrial Revolution. During this century many new art movements and styles emerged, with artists reflecting upon and responding to the changes around them. Romanticism began in this period and portrays strong emotions, feelings and moods. JMW Turner (1775–1851) was one of the masters of English Romantic painting. He was famous for his landscapes with dramatic sky effects and became known as 'the painter of light'.

Resources

- Pictures of Turner landscapes
- Cartridge paper
- Scissors
- Glue
- Photographs of dramatic sky effects

Approach

1 Introduce the children to this period in art by talking about the social and political revolutions of the time.
2 Show pictures of Turner landscapes such as *Calais Pier* and *The Fighting Téméraire.* Explain that Turner was fascinated by the play of light and creating different moods within his compositions.
3 Take or find several photographs of a dramatic sky effect. Have duplicates of each photograph printed to enable greater scope for cutting and sticking different areas.
4 Ask the children to lay their photographs, or parts of photographs, on a sheet of card to recreate a Turner-style sky.
5 Stick the images down firmly when all the prints are in position.

Monet Mono Prints

It is generally thought that modern art started in Paris in the mid-1880s with Impressionism, which had a major impact on western art. The painting *Impression, Sunrise* by Claude Monet (1840–1926) gave the Impressionist movement its name. Impressionist painters used strong colours and bold, broken brush strokes in their work. They painted outdoors because they wanted to show the effect of light and colour, giving the 'impression' of something. Monet was fascinated by the effects of light and how it changed the appearance of the same scene or pictorial object at different times of the day.

Resources

- Pictures of Monet's *Water Lilies*
- Sheets of transparent plastic
- Ready-mixed paint and brushes
- Cartridge paper
- Tissue paper

Approach

1 Look at pictures of Monet's series of paintings *Water Lilies*. Discuss the colours and mix poster paints to match the water lily pond. Pour the paint onto a sheet of transparent plastic and use a brush to roughly join the different colours together.
2 Carefully lower a sheet of cartridge paper onto the paint and press down firmly. Peel off the paper and allow to dry.
3 Refer back to the Monet paintings and add some detail in the form of cut tissue paper leaves and lily flowers.
4 Allow the plastic sheet to dry completely and the resulting image will provide a textured painting in its own right.

Cross-curricular Links

- **Literacy** – The Romantic movement included poets and writers. Look at the work of William Wordsworth (1770–1850), whose poetry was intrinsically linked to this period. Read *The Lady of Shallot* by Alfred, Lord Tennyson (1809–1892) and look at the Pre-Raphaelite painting of the same name by John William Waterhouse (1849–1917).
- **Geography** – Look at Monet's paintings entitled *Haystacks*. He painted the same scene at different times of the day and throughout different seasons. Provide examples of photographs of familiar scenes taken at different times of the day, or year. Ask the children to identify when they think they were taken by looking at the light effects. Take the children outside at different times of the day to observer the subtle light changes on a particular scene. Study the shapes and colours. Make notes and take photographs.

The Twentieth Century

Art Deco was a decorative style of art popular during the 1930s, in which the artists got their inspiration from many different sources including nature, ancient civilisation and other art movements. The style originated in Paris and was characterised by bold colours, geometric designs and stylised natural forms. Clarice Cliff (1899–1972) was an Art Deco artist famous for her bold-patterned, brightly coloured ceramics.

Clarice Cliff

Resources

- Pictures of ceramics by Clarice Cliff
- Balloons and papier-mâché
- Cardboard
- Paper
- Paint and brushes
- Paper plates

Approach

1 Show the children pictures of Clarice Cliff's ceramics. Discuss the geometric shapes and use of bold colours.
2 Cover balloons with papier-mâché (one between two children), allow to dry and then cut in two to make two vases. Attach pieces of cardboard to form the tops and bottoms of the vases.
3 Give the children a piece of paper to experiment with ideas for decoration based on the work of Clarice Cliff.
4 Invite them to transfer their designs onto the vase or plates cut out of circular pieces of card.

Andy Warhol

Andy Warhol (1928–87) was the most famous artist of the Pop Art movement. He created pictures using images from advertising, photography and the media. He called his studio 'The Factory', and from 1962 he stopped painting and began silk-screen printing instead. This method of producing pictures made each one slightly different and unique.

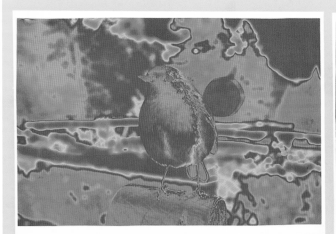

Resources

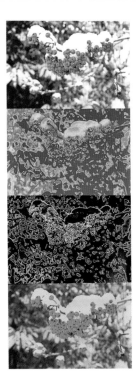

- Familiar household objects such as tins of soup, canned drinks and cereal packets
- Pictures of Andy Warhol's work
- Digital cameras
- Objects to photograph
- Computer and printer
- Photo-editing software

Approach

1 Explain to the children that Pop Art was inspired by the world of advertising. Provide a collection of familiar household objects with branding and packaging that the children will recognise. Alternatively, use objects around the school or scenes from nature.
2 Show pictures of Andy Warhol's work. Explain that he was a painter, graphic artist and film maker.
3 Use a digital camera to take photographs of the objects and upload them onto a computer.
4 Use a photo-editing software (such as Picnik, see www.picnik.com) to change the colours of the background to create Andy Warhol-type pictures.

Picasso's Weeping Woman

Pablo Picasso (1881–1973) was arguably the greatest artist of the 20th century. He was born in Malaga, Spain and was the son of a painter. He experimented with many different styles, constantly exploring new ideas and directions for painting and sculpture. He was a prolific artist and one of the leaders of the Cubist movement which lasted from 1907 to about 1922. He was an inventive sculptor and incorporated many different materials into his work.

Resources

- Pictures of Picasso's *Weeping Woman*
- Plastic masks (one per child)
- Sheets of cardboard (one per child)
- Paint, glue and collage materials

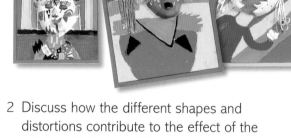

Approach

1 Show pictures of Picasso's *Weeping Woman*. Explain that from 1936 to 1939 there was a civil war in Pablo Picasso's native country, Spain, and that one of his most famous paintings *Guernica* was painted in response to the horrors of this war. *Weeping Woman* was part of a series of paintings also composed during this period and its deliberately distorted and exaggerated features express the fear and pain of war.

2 Discuss how the different shapes and distortions contribute to the effect of the painting. Talk about Picasso's use of vivid colour and how it contributes to the feeling of anguish.

3 Give the children cardboard, plastic masks, paints and collage materials and ask them to create a 3D version of the *Weeping Woman*.

Picasso's Sculptures

During the early 1960s, Picasso produced many sheet-metal sculptures. They link to Cubism and reveal his fascination with the relationship between form and space. Picasso was a pioneer of Cubism which is a style of painting that showed multiple viewpoints at the same time, and represents individual form as broken up into jagged, angular plains. Picasso made the sculptures in cardboard before turning them into more permanent sheet-metal sculptures.

Approach

1 Explain that Picasso's sheet-metal sculptures were made from thin metal about the thickness of an A4 sheet of paper. He made them during the 1960s. They were bent on two vertical lines, and Picasso first created models for his sculptures from card. Investigate how the sculptures link to his work on Cubism.

2 Show the children pictures of Picasso's sculptures and ask them to share their ideas about the inspiration behind them.

3 Give the children sheets of cardboard and give them time to experiment with different ways of folding, gluing and creating shapes out of cardboard to create a 3D sculpture.

4 Use thick silver card to make the final design then paint in black and white.

Resources

- Pictures of Picasso's sheet-metal sculptures
- Cardboard
- Scissors and glue
- Sheets of thick silver card
- Black and white poster paint

De Saint Phalle Sculptures

New Realism was an art movement that lasted from the middle of the 1950s into the 1970s. It is often seen as the European equivalent to Pop Art. The artists were interested in using mass-produced objects of everyday life and incorporating them into collages and assemblage. Niki de Saint Phalle (1930–2002) was a leading new realist. She was born in France but spend much of her life in America. She is perhaps best known for her brightly coloured figures of women that she called the 'nanas', inspired by the role of women in society. She made many different sculptures including a huge fountain sculpture named after the composer Igor Stravinsky which is situated in the middle of Paris next to the Pompidou Centre.

Resources

- Pictures of Niki de Saint Phalle's sculptures, including *Firebird*
- Stravinsky's *Firebird Suite* (optional)
- A version of the Russian folktale 'The Firebird' (optional)
- Cartridge paper and pencils
- Balloons and papier-mâché
- Scissors and glue
- Brightly coloured paints
- Mosaic pieces or collage materials
- Card

Approach

1 Show the children pictures of Niki de Saint Phalle's sculptures. Explain that they were made from a wire framework covered in papier-mâché. Discuss the inspiration for her *Firebird* sculpture. If possible, listen to excerpts from Stravinsky's *The Firebird* and read the Russian folktale it was based on.
2 Give the children paper and ask them to sketch out some ideas for their own firebird sculpture.
3 Use papier-mâchéd balloons to make the firebird 3D in parts.
4 Paint the firebird with brightly coloured poster paint and embellish with mosaic pieces.

Damien Hirst

Damien Hirst (1965–) is an English sculptor, painter, printmaker and installation artist. Installation art is art made of interesting materials, created and arranged for a specific space. One of his most famous pieces is a diamond-encrusted skull entitled *For the Love of God*. He said that the inspiration for this work came from seeing an Aztec skull covered in turquoise at the British Museum. Hirst used a real skull for his mould that is thought to have belonged to a person who lived in the 18th century. It cost £14 million to produce. He also has produced many 2D pieces of work and his spin paintings were created by placing canvas on a spinner and pouring on paint as it spins. The resulting pictures were given titles such as *Beautiful*, *Erupting*, *Shattering*, *Violent* and *Slashing*. His work is often controversial and challenges people to think about what is considered art.

Resources

- Pictures of Damien Hirst's work
- Cardboard mask
- Collage 'diamonds' (shiny embellishments) and sequins
- Glue and spreaders
- Perspex sheets

Approach

1 Explain that modern art often explores controversial ways of conveying ideas and can even be produced to shock or amuse. Look at the work of Damien Hirst and discuss the themes in his work and the materials he uses.

2 Talk about the inspiration behind the work entitled *For the Love of God*. Show the children a pictures of turquoise-covered Aztec skulls in the British Museum and discuss similarities and differences both in the making of the collage and the reasons they were made.

3 To make a diamond skull, spray a cardboard mask or 2D cardboard skull shape, with silver paint and glue on silver sequins and 'diamonds'.

4 To make the spin paintings, randomly cover a sheet of Perspex with brightly coloured poster paint and swirl a piece of paper around on top of it. Explain how Damien Hirst made his spin paintings and compare results. Give the pictures titles.

Cross-curricular Links

- **PSHE** – The 20th century brought with it many pioneering women artists including Mary Cassatt, Georgia O'Keeffe, Paula Rego to more recently Tracy Emin and Heather Lee Brent. Research the role of women in art and the changing social scene that made it possible for women to share equal access to the world of art. (One useful website is www.womenartists.co.uk.)

Islamic Art

Islam is the second largest religion on earth after Christianity, with more than one billion followers. Its followers are called Muslims and it was founded more than 1400 years ago by the prophet Muhammad. Islamic artists are forbidden to draw human figures or animals as the holy book the Qur'an teaches that only God is allowed to create and form living things. Islamic art is highly detailed and is characterised by complex geometric patterns.

Giant Islamic Tiles

Resources

- Examples of Islamic geometric tiles
- Ceramic tiles (one per child)
- Ceramic tile paints
- Squared paper
- Coloured crayons

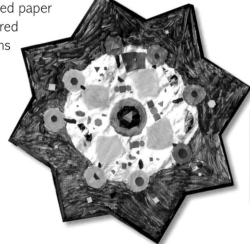

Approach

1 Show the children pictures of Islamic ceramic tiles and discuss how these are designed – many are based on the principles of symmetry. Look out for tessellating patterns and explain how this can be achieved.
2 Demonstrate using squared paper how these designs can be recreated.
3 Allow the children to experiment with ideas and, when they are happy with their design, transfer it onto a large sheet of cartridge paper. Paint and embellish with collage materials.

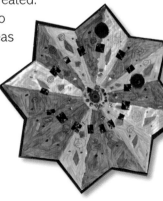

Islamic Calligraphy

Calligraphy is the art of beautiful and decorative writing and an important part of Islamic culture. In mosques throughout the world, Arabic script, often taken from the Qur'an, is used as decoration, and Muslims have become famous for their calligraphy and manuscript illumination. Arabic is the language of Islam and the Qur'an. It is read from right to left and consists of 28 basic letters. Religious inscriptions were first written on paper or parchment but, later on, tiles, pottery, embroidery, vases, prayer mats and wall carpets were decorated in beautiful ornate calligraphy. Well-used phrases and verses from the Qur'an have been made into shapes or patterns.

Resources

- Examples of Islamic calligraphy and calligrams
- A copy of the Arabic alphabet
- Examples of well-known Arabic phrases or greetings
- Ceramic tiles
- Ceramic paints and outliners

Approach

1 Explain to the children that many Islamic calligraphers produced calligrams, pictures made from words. Show examples of calligrams, where the Arabic language has been shaped into pictures or patterns.
2 Show examples of the Arabic alphabet and well known phrases or Eid greetings. Encourage the children to practise drawing letters or phrases.
3 Invite them to transfer their designs onto ceramic tiles using outliners. When the outlines are dry, they can be filled in with ceramic paints.

Ottoman Iznik Ceramics

The Ottoman Empire was famous for its Iznik ceramics. The pottery was named after the town Iznik, south-west of Istanbul, where it was made. The potteries flourished during the late 15th century and originally the ceramic ware was white, decorated in blue. It was influenced by the blue and white porcelain of Ming dynasty China. By the mid-16th century the range of colours had increased to include turquoise, green and red. Bowls, jugs, vases and flat dishes were made and the designs were mainly plant and flower shapes.

Resources

- Balloons and papier-mâché
- Cardboard
- Pictures of Iznik ceramics
- Paper
- Turquoise, blue, green and red paints and brushes
- Silk-screen and squeegee
- A3 paper
- Fabric

Approach

1 To make a vase, blow up a balloon and cover it with papier-mâché. Allow to dry. Cut the balloon in half and make a stand for the vase out of cardboard. Glue the stand in place.

2 Look at pictures of Iznik ceramics and invite the children to sketch out some ideas for designs, then paint the bowl in turquoise, blue and green.

3 To make an Iznik-style screen print, prepare a stencil by drawing a pattern inspired by the Iznik ceramics onto a sheet of A3 paper. Shade the stencil in black and white. (The black areas will be printed in one colour; the white areas will be another colour.) Photocopy the stencil twice.

4 Cut out the black shapes on one of the photocopies and discard the rest of the paper. Place the stencil on a sheet of fabric, lower the screen over the top and use a squeegee to pull green or blue paint evenly from the top of the screen to the bottom. This may take two or three pulls.

5 Remove the screen. The paper stencil should stick to the screen, leaving the background painted. Clean the screen and allow the fabric to dry.

6 Cut out the white shapes on the second stencil and place in position on top of the printed fabric. Repeat the printing process with the other colour.

7 The design can be enhanced by adding appliquéd or painted red flowers.

Ottoman Marbling

Marbling is the art of creating patterns by sprinkling colour on oily water and then placing a sheet of paper on top to absorb the dye and 'print' the pattern. The Turkish art of Ebru (marbling) was developed in Istanbul more than 500 years ago. Traditionally, Ebru paper was used to create decorative book covers that were also decorated with various forms of Islamic script.

Resources

- Water tray
- Marbling inks
- Cartridge paper
- Examples of Ottoman marbling papers
- Paints and brushes

Approach

1 Fill a tray with water and demonstrate the process of creating swirling patterns by dropping marbling ink into the water and moving it in circular movements. Place a sheet of cartridge paper on top of the water to 'print' the marbling pattern. Allow to dry.

2 Look at examples of Ottoman marbling papers. Many have been decorated with patterns and pictures of flowers. Remind the children that pictures of animals and human figures were not common in Ottoman art and often the papers were just covers with script or decorative patterns.

3 Use the marbled paper to make book covers.

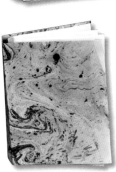

Cross-curricular Links

- **Religious education** – Research the festival of Eid ul-Fitr. It marks the end of Ramadan when Muslims do not eat or drink during daylight hours. The date of this festival varies according to the Islamic lunar calendar. Muslims send out greeting cards, exchange presents and have Eid parties with special foods.

- **Maths** – Using squared paper, design geometric patterns with a specific mathematical focus, for example, ones that tessellate, symmetrical designs, ones with rotational symmetry, ones that use squares, equilateral triangles, regular hexagons and so on.

Japanese Art

Japan has a long history of art that stretches back to ancient times. There are many different periods of Japanese history covering many different styles and media, all communicating something different about Japanese life and its distinctive character. Although it was greatly influenced by Chinese styles, the arts and crafts of Japan have developed a strong identity of their own with all things in nature being a major inspiration. Woodblock printing was first used in Japan to print religious texts. Woodblocks in the 17th century were known as *ukiyo-e* which literally means 'floating world'. Hokusai (1760–1849) was one of the leading ukiyo-e painters. He created thousands of prints but the most famous were probably from the series entitled *Thirty-six Views of Mount Fuji.*

Woodblock Prints

Resources

- Picture of Hokusai's woodcut prints, including *The Great Wave off Kanagawa*
- Paint and rollers
- Cartridge paper
- Polystyrene press print sheets

Approach

1 Look at examples of Hokusai's woodcut prints. Explain the history of the technique and how it was a cheap way to reproduce art.

2 Show the children a picture of Hokusai's *The Great Wave off Kanagawa* and draw their attention to the boats in the picture.

3 Sketch the boats on a piece of paper and then reproduce the image onto a piece of press print, using a sharp pencil. Demonstrate the pressure required to achieve a clear print without going through the polystyrene.

4 Apply the paint to the print sheet using the roller dipped in paint and press it firmly onto a sheet of paper to make a print. Use wooden matchsticks to print on the spray.

5 Make a 3D copy of *The Great Wave off Kanagawa* and attach the printed boats to the picture.

6 Hokusai's work influenced many artists. Research the work of the Impressionist painter Claude Monet and discuss the Japanese influence.

Japanese Kites

The Japanese have a long history of kite flying and it is thought that Buddhist monks brought kites to Japan in the 7th century. They were probably flown for religious purposes to frighten away evil spirits and to bring good fortune and ensure rich harvests. Nowadays kite flying is an important part of festivals and religious holidays. Children's Day is a Japanese festival celebrated in Japan on 5 May every year. Traditionally it was called Boy's Day but it now celebrates the happiness of all children. On this day, carp kites that symbolise strength, determination and courage are flown outside Japanese homes. The carp kites are called *Koinobori* and are usually decorated with red or blue patterns.

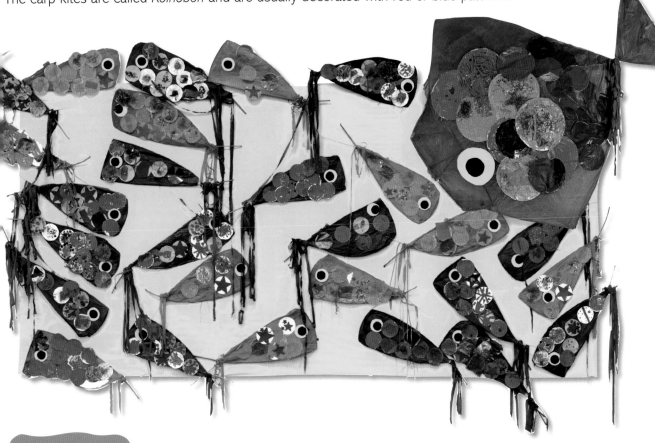

Resources

- Withy canes and masking tape
- PVA glue and sponges
- Crêpe tissue
- Foil paper
- Collage material, including sequins

Approach

1 Using one piece of cane, bend it round to make a fish shape and join together with masking tape.
2 Mix PVA glue with water in a bowl and use a sponge to carefully cover a sheet of crêpe paper with glue.
3 Drape the tissue paper over the withy cane frame, and cover with another layer of the PVA mixture so that the crêpe paper dries hard.
4 Cut out scales in different papers and embellish with sequins and other collage material.
5 Make streamers from the crêpe paper and glue everything together.

Noh Masks

The origins of Noh theatre go back to the 14th century and can be traced back to the religious dances that took place outside Buddhist temples. Noh performers combine poetry, dance and music to tell their stories. Masks are worn by the main characters. These are carved from wood and then painted. There are many different masks and they can depict a variety of emotions depending on how the actor moves his head or the direction from which the audience views them.

Resources

- Video of a Noh play (optional)
- Pictures of Noh masks
- Balloons and papier-mâché, or plastic masks
- Cartridge paper
- Paint and brushes

Approach

1 Talk to the children about traditional Japanese theatre. Explain that Noh performances are based on strong Zen Buddhist principles of restraint, understatement, sparing use of movement and frugality of expression. If possible, provide a video of a Noh play and discuss these principles.

2 Blow up a balloon and cover with several layers of papier-mâché. When dry, pop the balloon and cut in half to make two masks.

3 Look at the examples of masks and discuss the choice of colours, shapes, expressions and so on. Ask the children to sketch out some ideas on a piece of cartridge paper, then to paint and decorate the masks.

4 Prepare a Noh play or dance and wear the masks in a performance.

Origami Flowers

Origami is the art of paper folding. It is a Japanese compound word, *ori* means 'to fold' and *kami* means 'paper'.

Resources

- Origami paper

Approach

1 Demonstrate how to make an origami flower:

a Fold a square piece of paper in half diagonally.

b Find the middle point on the folded edge by folding the triangle in half and pressing down lightly at the bottom.

c Unfold and with a finger on the middle point, lift up one pointed edge and fold it so it lies sloping upwards. Repeat with the other side.

2 Encourage children to experiment with other ways of making flowers and leaves.

Japanese Fans

The folded fan was invented by the Japanese. Two of the most commonly used materials in Japanese art are paper and silk, and fans are often made out of these. Cherry blossom, the national flower of Japan, is often chosen as a decorative motif.

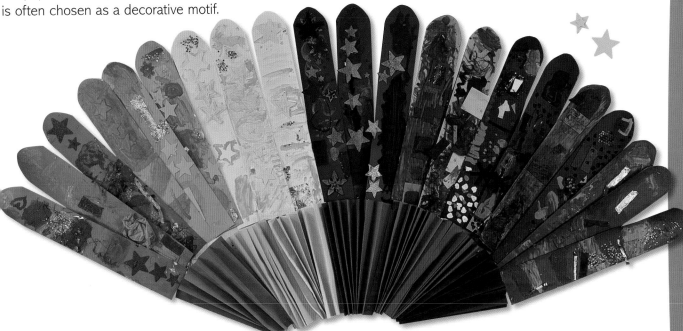

Resources

- Pictures of Japanese fans
- Rectangular pieces of card in the colours of the rainbow
- Paints and brushes
- Collage materials
- Glue and scissors

Approach

1 Show the children pictures of Japanese fans. Discuss the motifs and the colours that are used.
2 Provide each child with a rectangular sheet of card and allocate them a colour of the rainbow. Talk to the children about primary and secondary colours.
3 Discuss ways of decorating their individual part of the fan using the paints and available collage material.
4 Display as a giant rainbow fan.

Cross-curricular Links

- **Art** – Study the work of Isamu Noguchi (1904–1988), a sculptor who spent most of his childhood in Japan. Look at a piece entitled *Noh Musicians*. It is made of steel, a solid, inflexible material but represents music, which is fluid and flexible. Discuss the obvious contradictions and speculate on Noguchi's reason for this choice of material.
- **Literacy** – Write Haiku poetry. It consists of 17 syllables divided between three lines. The first line contains five syllables, the second line seven and the third line five. The subject for Haiku should be uncomplicated and describe an experience most people can relate to. A traditional Haiku often describes something in nature.

Native North American Art

The native peoples of the north-western United States and Canada were expert carvers. They carved totem poles from giant cedar trees and showed pictures of creatures such as killer whales, grizzly bears and birds. They were placed in front of wooden lodges and depicted a family history of the tribes and families who lived there. The poles showed the status and rank of the family as well as commemorating their ancestors and their sacred protectors.

Approach

1　Show the children pictures of Native American totem poles. Encourage the children to engage with the pictures by asking some questions, for example: *What materials do you think have been used to make the totem pole? How do you think it was made? How big do you think it is? Can you tell what the pole is portraying?*

2　Talk about the significance of the images and ask for suggestions as to what the children might depict on a pole outside their family home. (Alternatively, think about a school totem pole.)

3　Give the children a long thin sheet of cartridge paper. Remind the children that the totem pole told a visual story about the tribe or family who owned it. What story would they tell about their family or school to pass down to future generations? Ask the children to sketch out their own totem pole.

4　Using cardboard tubes and sheets of cardboard, demonstrate how to create some of the shapes they have drawn on their plans.

5. Paint the totem poles in bright colours.

Totem Poles

Resources

- Pictures of totem poles
- Large sheets of cartridge paper, cut in half to make two long, thin sheets
- Cardboard tubes
- Paint and brushes
- Pencils
- Glue and spreaders

Buffalo Robe Paintings

Buffalo robes were worn by the Indians of the Northern Plains. The designs documented scenes from individual lives and were made for both practical and ceremonial purposes. Geometric designs were common and each colour and shape had a meaning.

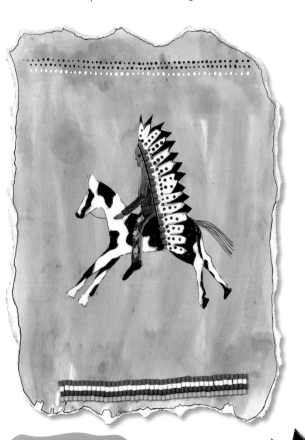

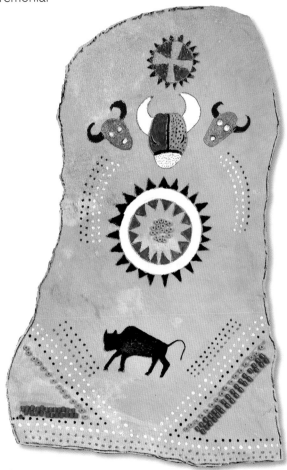

Resources

- Chamois leather
- Cartridge paper
- Cold wet tea bags
- Pictures of buffalo hide drawings
- Felt pens

Approach

1. Give the children the opportunity to feel the texture of 'hide' in the form of chamois leather.
2. To make paper that looks like buffalo hide, soak a tea bag in water and 'wash' over a piece of cartridge paper. Allow to dry and tear round the edges.
3. Show pictures of buffalo hide drawings. Explain that they often depicted important personal experiences. Encourage the children to experiment with designs that represent a story or event from their own life.
4. Let them draw their designs in pencil and colour them in with felt pens on the buffalo hide paper.

47

Navajo Sand Painting

The Navajo people moved to the south-west part of North America from their home in Canada around 1400CE. They are one of the largest surviving Native American tribes. Their sand paintings were created by medicine men as part of a healing ceremony. These paintings are made on the floor of a hut or on animal skins. The medicine man draws the different spirits of animals and plants that have special healing powers. The healing ceremony lasts many days and when the ritual is over, the sand painting is swept away. The paintings can range in size and are made from natural coloured soil and sand.

Resources

- Pictures of Navajo sand paintings
- Cardboard
- White, blue, yellow and black powder paint
- Glue   • Sand

Approach

1 Explain the history of the Navajo people and show pictures of the sand paintings that are made out of different coloured sand for healing ceremonies.

2 Using the pictures as examples, ask the children to sketch out a design on a piece of cardboard.

3 Provide four pots of sand and mix dry powder paint with the sand in the four main colours of white, blue, yellow and black.

4 Spread glue and sprinkle the coloured sand onto the appropriate areas using one colour at a time.

Navajo Rugs

The Navajo people learned techniques for weaving on a loom from their Pueblo neighbours.
The men would pick and spin the cotton but it was usually dyed and woven by women. The rugs are
characterised by complex geometric patterns.

Resources

- Pictures of Navajo rugs
- Squared paper
- Coloured sheets of thin foam
- Scissors and glue

Approach

1 Show the children pictures of Navajo rugs
   and identify all the geometric shapes and the
   symmetry within the designs.
2 Provide squared paper and demonstrate how
   to create a simple symmetrical geometric
   design.
3 Transfer ideas onto a sheet of foam.
4 Put all the designs together and create a
   group rug.

49

Corn Husk Dolls

According to Iroquois legend the 'Sustainers of Life', also known as 'The Three Sisters', are corn, beans and squash. The legend goes that the corn spirit was so delighted at being one of the important sustainers of life that she asked the Creator what more she could do for the people. The Creator said that a beautiful doll could be made from her husks for the children to play with. At first, the doll that was made from the corn husk played nicely with the children and helped to look after them. She was very beautiful and everyone adored her but, after seeing her reflection in the water, all she thought about was her beautiful face and she became very vain. The Creator warned her to be good otherwise he would punish her but, even though she promised to be humble, she carried on as normal. One afternoon, she was walking by the creek and stopped to look at her beautiful reflection. The Creator decided to teach her a lesson and sent a giant screech owl out of the sky to snatch her reflection from the water. When she looked in the water again she saw she had no reflection. When an Iroquois mother makes a doll for her children she tells this story to remind them that the child is no better than anyone else, and that the Creator has given a special gift to everyone.

Approach

1. Tell the children the story of the corn husk doll.
2. Explain that the dolls are often made without faces and ask them why they think that this is so.
3. Demonstrate how to tie the raffia into a shape of a doll and fasten with elastic bands. Experiment with plaiting raffia to make the arms and legs.
4. Use the doll as a puppet to re-tell the story of the corn husk doll.

Resources

- Raffia
- String
- Scissors

Chilkat Weaving

Chilkat weaving is a traditional form of weaving practised by the north-west coastal tribes of Alaska and British Columbia. High ranking tribal members wore the blankets at ceremonial occasions. It is arguably one of the most complex weaving techniques in the world and one blanket can take as long as a year to weave. The blankets are made from goat wool, dog fur and yellow cedar bark. The blankets depict clan crests and figures from their oral history. They are often pictures of animals or facial features. Yellow and black are dominant colours. It was said that if you knew how to listen, the faces on the blanket could talk. They were prized possessions and when the owners died, they would be buried in them.

Resources

- Pictures of Chilkat blankets
- Cartridge paper
- Coloured felt in yellow, black and white
- Glue   • Scissors

Approach

1 Show the children pictures of Chilkat blankets and talk about the shapes and colours.
2 Provide paper and pencils and ask the children to design a clan crest for a blanket then to create it from felt.
3 Put all the crests together to make a blanket.

Cross-curricular Links

- **Maths** – Wampum were small beads made from polished shells and used by some North American people as currency. Discuss currencies throughout history and today.
- **Science** – In 1492, there were several million Native Americans living in North America. By the late 1880s, the population had been reduced to around 280,000. The main reason for the death toll were European diseases that the Native Americans had no resistance to. Research smallpox, influenza, whooping cough and measles and find out how we protect ourselves from them nowadays.
- **Music** – Rainsticks are ceremonial instruments to invoke the rain spirits. Design and make some Native American rainsticks.

Mexican and Central American Art

Mexico's history goes back thousands of years and can be broadly divided into two main periods: Pre-Hispanic (1200BCE–1519CE) and Post-Conquest (1519CE–present day). The Pre-Hispanic period includes the ancient civilisations of the Mayans and the Aztecs. The Mayans are renowned for the cities they built with amazing pyramids. The Aztecs flourished during a later period between the 14th and 16th centuries but were conquered by the Spanish conquistador Hernán Cortés (1485–1547) in 1519.

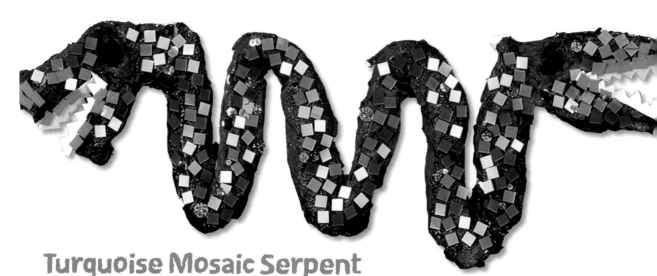

Turquoise Mosaic Serpent

Resources

- Newspaper
- Mod-Roc
- Turquoise paint and brushes
- Turquoise mosaic pieces or shells
- Glue and glue spreaders

Approach

1 Explain to the children a brief history of Mexico. Draw a timeline and put on key dates.
2 Explain that double-headed and entwined serpents were common symbols in Mesoamerican art. They are thought to represent the sky, and the habit of snakes shedding their skin each year symbolises renewal and transformation. Show a picture of the double-headed serpent turquoise mosaic that dates back to the 15th or 16th century, and explain that it would probably have been amongst the treasures given by the emperor Moctezuma to Hernán Cortés upon his arrival on the coast of Mexico in 1519. The serpent mosaic is made from wood which has been hollowed out at the back and covered completely with turquoise, red and white shell. It was probably made as an ornament to be worn at the back of a headdress or a pectoral (chest ornament).
3 Shape some newspaper into the form of a serpent.
4 Cover the serpent in Mod-Roc and allow to dry.
5 Paint the whole model in turquoise paint.
6 Decorate in turquoise mosaic and shells.

The Day of the Dead

The Day of the Dead festival can be traced back to the time of the Aztecs where a month-long summer festival was dedicated to a goddess called Mictecacihutl or 'Lady of the Dead'. When the Aztecs were conquered by Spain more than 500 years ago, they changed the festival to early November to coincide with All Saints' Day of the Catholic Church. Nowadays the festival is a mixture of cultures combining traditional native and Catholic beliefs. It is a time when the spirits of the deceased are thought to be reunited with their families. The spirits are welcomed back with offerings of food and other things that the person enjoyed in life, all laid out on beautifully decorated altars in the family home. It is not a sombre occasion but a time for feasting and celebration. A common symbol of the festival is the skull, and sugar skulls are placed at the altar, often with the deceased person's name inscribed at the top. It is a joyous occasion and a time to remember loved ones who have died.

Resources

- Cardboard masks (one per child)
- Cardboard
- Cartridge paper
- Paint and brushes
- Glue and spreaders
- Collage materials, including foil and sugar craft flowers

Approach

1 Tell the children about the history of the festival of the Day of the Dead, and explain how sugar skulls are a traditional folk art from southern Mexico used to celebrate this day. The skulls are decorated with icing, pieces of bright foil and coloured sugar flowers.

2 Attach the cardboard masks onto a sheet of cardboard using small strips of sticky tape.

3 Invite the children to sketch out a design on paper and transfer their ideas onto the mask.

4 When dry, the masks can be embellished with foil, sugar flowers and sequins.

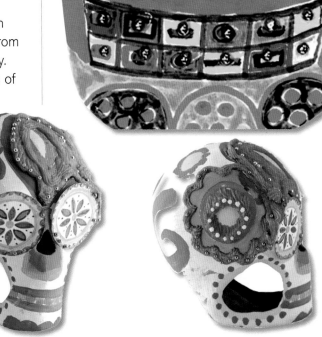

Kuna Molas

Molas are appliquéd textiles made by the Kuna Indians of the San Blas islands of Panama, Central America. They are made by building up several layers of brightly coloured cloth. Some parts of the design are stitched together and others are cut out to expose underlying colours. Designs can be inspired by the natural world or be purely abstract. The finished molas form part of the traditional costume worn by the Kuna women.

Resources

- A world map
- Pictures of molas
- Felt or, for younger children, coloured pieces of craft foam
- Scissors • Glue

Approach

1 Locate Central America and Panama on a world map. Explain to the children a little about the Kuna Indians and their way of life.

2 Show pictures of molas and discuss how they are made.

3 Encourage the children to sketch out ideas on a piece of paper and demonstrate how to cut out their design and use it as a stencil to create the same design in felt or foam.

4 Invite them to add layers to their designs. With older children, encourage them to cut out areas and use stitches to embellish their pattern.

Huichol Art

The Huichol are one of Mexico's indigenous peoples and are renowned for their brightly coloured yarn paintings and patterned beadwork. Huichol artists have been producing art for thousands of years, and use nature and the world around them as their inspiration. Every piece of art has spiritual significance. Art is also a form of prayer and a way of communicating with their ancestors and gods.

Resources

- Pictures of Huichol yarn paintings and beaded bowls
- Square pieces of cardboard (one per child)
- PVA glue and spreaders
- Brightly coloured yarn
- Paints and brushes
- Plastic plates or bowls (one per child)
- Round pieces of cartridge paper
- Coloured beads
- Papier-mâché

Approach

1 Introduce the topic by explaining the history of the Huichol people and locating north-west Mexico on a map. Show the children examples of Huichol yarn paintings. Tell them that the symbols are an important form of communication and that they have a religious significance. Use the internet to research Huichol symbols and see if the children can identify any of the symbols in the examples.

2 Give each child a square piece of cardboard and ask them to design their own yarn painting. Discuss the use of colour and paint in brightly coloured poster paint. Demonstrate how to cover in areas with strips of yarn.

3 Show the children pictures of beaded bowls. Provide the children with plastic plates or bowls to cover in papier-mâché. Allow the bowls to dry.

4 Ask the children to sketch out a design on a piece of paper. Let them transfer their ideas onto the inside of the bowls. They should paint the bowls in brightly coloured poster paint, choosing a small area to cover in beads.

Cross-curricular Links

- **Literacy** – The concept of balance in nature is central to Huichol art and culture, and the balancing of opposites such as summer and winter, night and day is a common theme. Discuss opposites in nature and compose verses inspired by contrasting pairs, for example, a moonlit night and a snowy morning.

Chinese Art

Chinese history stretches back more than 10,000 years, and periods of history are often referred to in dynasties. The earliest records of paper exist from China in 105BCE under the Han dynasty and Emperor Han Wu-ti (140–87BCE). It was made from a mixture including hemp, rags and mulberry tree bark, pounded together with water. After being laid out onto a bamboo mat to filter away the water, the mixture was dried and pressed. Chinese painting dates back more than 3000 years to the Shang dynasty (16th to 11th century BCE) but it wasn't until around the 13th century BCE that artists began to paint on paper. During the Yuan dynasty (1271–1368BCE), painters developed the 'mind landscape' style of painting. It expressed personal feelings and conveyed the inner landscape of the spirit and soul.

Chinese Paper-Making and Painting

Resources

- World map
- Scrap paper
- Bucket, water, blender and plastic tray
- Frame around which a wire mesh is stretched
- Plasticine®

Approach

1 Locate China on a world map and talk to the children about the Chinese dynasties. Explain that since 1949 it has been a communist country. Explain what this means.

2 Tell the children the history of paper-making.

3 Tear the scrap paper into small pieces. Put the paper into a bucket, cover the paper with water and leave overnight.

4 Remover the pulp and put in a blender. Add water so that the blender is three quarters full and blend together. Pour into a plastic tray and add water, one part pulp to four parts water. Pour over the mesh and allow the water to drain away. Allow the paper to dry, then press under heavy books.

5 Let the children use the paper to paint some 'mind landscape' paintings. They could add calligraphy, and design and print a personal seal out of Plasticine®.

Willow Pattern Plate

The first porcelain came from China and dates back to around 700ce. China produced arguably the best porcelain in the world and, as the centuries passed, pottery became known throughout Europe as 'Fine China' or 'China'. Porcelain is made from fine whitish clay called kaolin that becomes hard, glossy and almost translucent when fired in a kiln. The different provinces in China all produced their own unique styles and the famous blue and white porcelain started in a town called Jingdezhen. By the beginning of the 17th century it was being exported to Europe. The famous willow pattern was probably made at an English factory in Staffordshire and the design is attributed to a Chinese legend about a pair of star-crossed lovers.

Resources

- The story of the willow pattern, for example *The Willow Pattern Story* by Allan Drummond (North-South Books, 1995)
- A picture of a willow pattern plate
- Circular pieces of card
- Circular pieces of silk
- Silk gutta
- Silk paints

Approach

1 Read the story of the willow pattern and show the children a picture of a willow pattern plate. Can the children identify the different elements of the story in the picture?
2 Explain to the children the history of porcelain and explain that China had an important role in the development of both porcelain ware and silk manufacture.

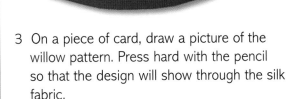

3 On a piece of card, draw a picture of the willow pattern. Press hard with the pencil so that the design will show through the silk fabric.
4 Place the silk on top of the design and tape round the edges.
5 Trace around the lines of the drawing in silk gutta, making sure that the gutta completely encloses areas of the silk.
6 Paint the designs with silk paints and leave to dry.
7 Gently peel off the silk from the cardboard and mount on a new piece of card.

Chinese New Year Lion

At Chinese New Year, one of the traditional dances performed for good luck is the lion dance. The giant lion masks are made from a bamboo frame and paper, and the costume is traditionally made from silk with coloured tassels. According to Chinese legend, Chinese New Year began with a fight against a mythical beast called the Nian. Once a year, it would enter villages and devour crops, livestock and even children. A wise man suggested that the people should make lion masks to frighten the beast away. The people believed that the Nian was also afraid of the colour red and loud noises, so started wearing red robes and using firecrackers to scare him away.

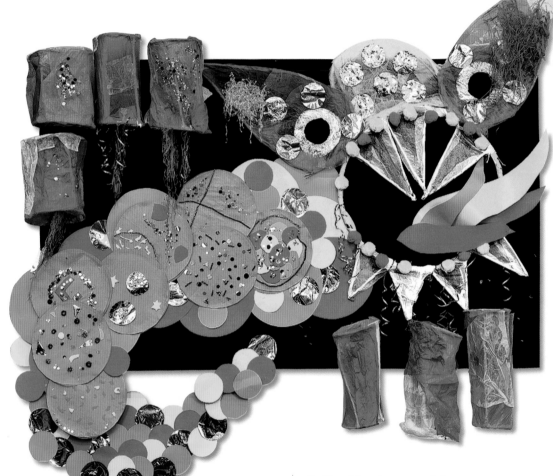

Resources

- The story of the Chinese zodiac (optional)
- Pictures of Chinese New Year lions
- Cartridge paper
- Withy canes
- Masking tape
- PVA glue and bowl
- Sponges
- Tissue paper

Approach

1 If possible, set the scene for this activity by telling the children the story of the Chinese Zodiac. (For an illustrated version, visit www.topmarks.co.uk and search for 'Zodiac Story'.)

2 Provide pictures of Chinese New Year lions for inspiration and to sketch out some ideas.

3 Soak the withy canes in water for an hour or so to make them more pliable.

4 Demonstrate how to bend the canes to make a frame for the lion's head. Fasten the canes together with masking tape. Make a mixture of PVA glue and water in a bowl and use a sponge to carefully cover a sheet of tissue paper with the glue.

5 Drape the tissue paper over the withie frame and cover with another layer of the PVA mixture so that the tissue paper dries hard.

6 Embellish with collage materials.

7 Make the lion's costume by decorating circles of cartridge paper with tassels and sequins.

...mes with brightly coloured lanterns. The celebrations end ...rn festival.

...shapes and colours.

2 Soak the withy canes in water for an hour or so to make them more pliable.
3 Demonstrate how to bend the canes into the shape of a lantern and secure different parts with masking tape.
4 Make a mix of PVA glue and water in a bowl and use a sponge to carefully cover a sheet of tissue paper with the glue mixture.
5 Drape the tissue paper over the withie cane frame and cover with another layer of the PVA mixture so that the tissue paper dries hard.
6 When the lanterns are dry, the children can decorate them with Chinese writing and patterns.

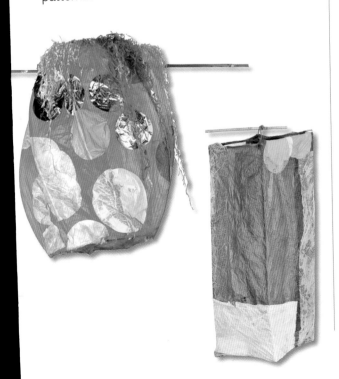

Cross-curricular Links

● **RE** – The 'Diamond Sutra' scroll is the world's earliest dated printed book. It was made in 868CE and is an important sacred text for the Buddhist faith. Find out more about the scroll, including where and when it was found. Copy part of the scroll onto commercially bought handmade paper, then add to your display.

59

Indian Art

Mehndi Patterns

Women celebrate festivals like Diwali and celebrations in India by applying henna designs to their hands and feet. The henna dye is reddish brown in colour and used to paint beautiful intricate patterns onto the body. The designs often incorporate India's national bird, the peacock, and the lotus flower, which is India's national flower.

Resources

- Images of simple mehndi patterns
- Tissue paper
- Cartridge paper
- Ink pens and ink or felt pens
- Sequins and embroidery mirrors

Approach

1 Place a sheet of tissue paper on top of a piece of white cartridge paper so the children's designs can be easily seen.
2 Ask the children to draw around their hand onto the tissue paper and then, using ink pens and ink (or felt pens), design a pattern on the hand shape. Encourage them to make their designs as elaborate as possible.

4 Allow the ink to dry, then add sequins and embroidery mirrors to embellish the designs.
5 Display the decorated hands overlapping each other to create a see-through pattern.

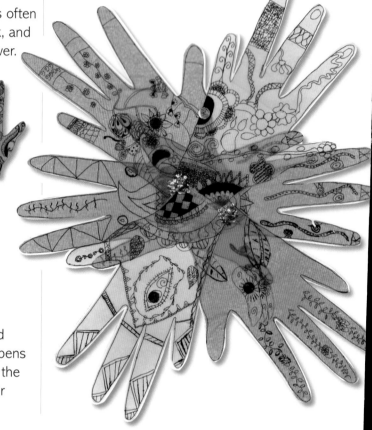

Ganesha Models

Hinduism is an Indian religion and Ganesha is one of the best-known Hindu gods. He has an elephant head and a huge belly due to his fondness for sweets. There are many different versions of how he got his elephant head but, according to one, Ganesha's mother Parvati made her son out of clay from the Ganges River. When her husband, the god Shiva, arrived home, Ganesha wouldn't allow him in, so angry Shiva struck off his head. To save him, Shiva agreed to give him the head of the first animal to pass, which happened to be a wise elephant. Hindus celebrate Ganesha's birthday every year and children make clay models of the holy elephant.

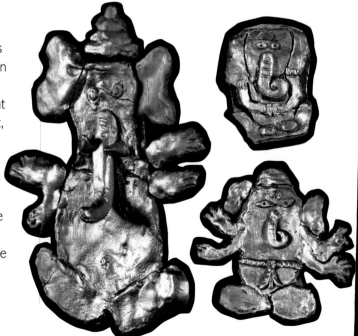

Tie-Dye

Tie-dyeing is a method of dyeing cloth that is widely used in India. The cloth is covered in many tiny little dots formed by tying off little circles of cloth with thread.

Resources

- Circles of cotton fabric
- Dried peas
- Elastic bands
- An iron
- Coloured dye
- Thick cardboard
- Paints
- Pictures of traditional Indian motifs
- Little embroidery mirrors
- Coloured embroidery thread and needles

Approach

1   Demonstrate how to create small circular tie-dye patterns by tying dried peas into the fabric randomly using elastic bands, then dyeing the fabric. When the fabric is dry, take off the elastic bands and iron flat.
2   Make a block print out of cardboard. Look at traditional Indian motifs and make sketches, then transfer the designs onto pieces of cardboard and cut them out.
3   Stick the shape onto another piece of card and allow to dry.
4   When the block is ready, apply paint and press onto the cloth.
5   Decide where to put the mirrors and attach with embroidery thread.

Resources

- Pictures of Ganesha
- Air-hardening clay and clay tools
- Gold spray or paint
- Sequins

Approach

1   Read the story of how Ganesha got his elephant head. Explain that many people worship him in temples because they believe he is wise and can help them when starting something new.
2   Show pictures and make preliminary sketches of the elephant god.
3   Give each child some air-hardening clay and demonstrate how to sculpt and join the clay.
4   Spray or paint gold and make a necklace out of sequins for the sculpture.

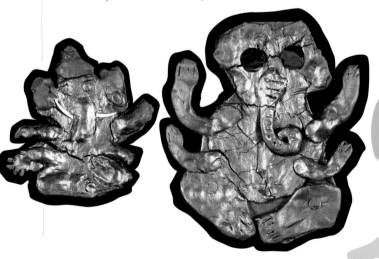

Block Prints

India is renowned for its beautiful block-printed cloth. The designs are carved out of wooden blocks and different areas of the country have different colour schemes and designs. It is a long process of decorating cloth as the block needs to be carved and used to print many times to create the entire design. Sometimes several different blocks are used and, if different colours are going to be used, a separate block must be made for each colour.

Resources

- Pictures of Indian block-printed cloth
- Plasticine®   ● Clay tools
- Cardboard and PVA glue
- Black paint and brushes
- Handmade paper or wrapping paper with a simple pattern

Approach

1 Look at different examples of Indian block printed cloth. Discuss the designs and shapes used.

2 The mango shape is a popular image and an easy one for children to carve out of Plasticine®. Sketch out a shape and demonstrate how to transfer and carve out the design.

3 Stick the Plasticine® shape onto a piece of cardboard using PVA glue. Allow to dry.

4 Paint the raised Plasticine® shape with black paint and press down firmly on the paper to make a clear impression.

5 Experiment with different repeating patterns.

Indian Batiks

Batik refers to the art of dyeing fabric by using a wax-resist technique. India has a long and rich tradition of batik work. There are many different themes from religious paintings to abstract designs and the fabrics used are cotton and silk. India is one of the top producers of silk in the world.

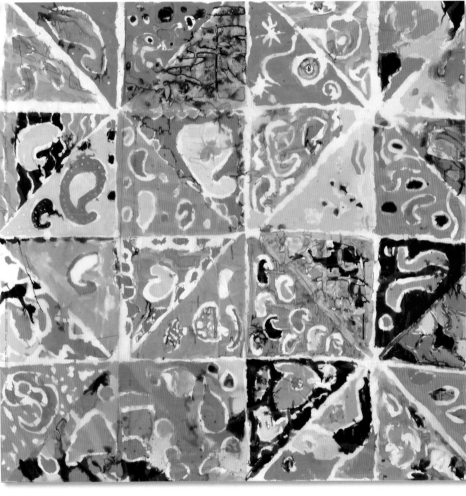

Resources

- Pictures of batiks from India
- Cartridge paper
- Silk fabric
- Cold batik
- Silk paints
- An iron and kitchen roll

Approach

1 Look at batiks from India. Discuss the patterns and colours used. Ask the children to sketch out a pattern or picture based on the examples. The mango motif is a popular one in Indian textiles.

2 When the children are happy with the design, cover the paper with a sheet of silk and use a brush to apply a layer of wax on the areas that are to be kept white.

3 Allow to dry and paint the remaining areas in silk paints.

4 Adult help will be needed to iron off the wax between layers of kitchen roll.

Cross-curricular Links

- **Literacy/Design and technology** – A kavad is a small storytelling box often made from wood. The boxes depict stories from Hindu mythology. They are brightly painted with images from stories and contain lots of secret compartments that, when opened up, reveal more and more of the story. Show pictures of the storytelling boxes. Look at the pictures and shapes, and discuss how they are made. Demonstrate how to make basic pop-up book constructions, flaps, concertina books and so on. Provide a variety of model-making materials and ask the children to design and make a storytelling box with hidden compartments. Tell the story of Rama and Sita and write the story in the box.

African Art

The people of Ghana in West Africa make a cloth called Adinkra. The symbols that decorate the cloth are carved onto a stamp made from pieces of calabash or gourd. There are many different symbols and each one has a different meaning. The word Adinkra means 'goodbye' and, traditionally, Adinkra was worn by kings and tribal leaders at funeral services. Originally the colours would have been red, russet brown, terracotta, black and white. In modern times, Adinkra cloth comes in many bright colours and is worn by everyone at special occasions such as festivals, weddings and naming ceremonies.

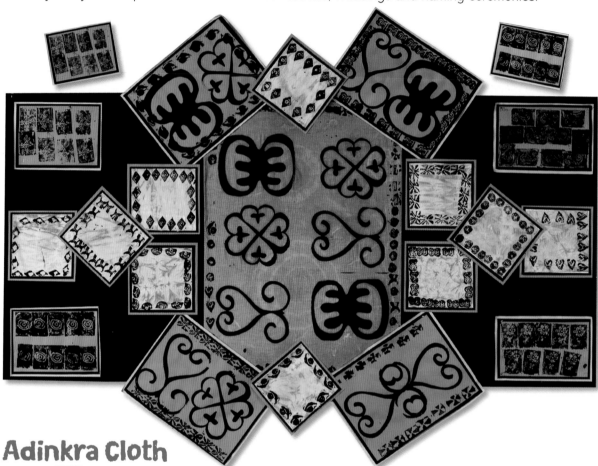

Adinkra Cloth

Resources

- Pictures of Adinkra symbols
- Plasticine®
- Scissors or craft tools
- Rectangular pieces of cloth (one per child)
- Coloured cold water dye
- An iron
- Thick poster paint and brushes

Approach

1 Tell the children about the background of Adinkra cloth and explain that each symbol has a name and a meaning.

2 Show examples of Adinkra symbols and ask the children to choose one that has a message that is significant to them or has a message they would like to convey.

3. Invite them to draw a design onto a piece of Plasticine® and demonstrate how to cut away the background safely by using a craft tool.

4. Dye pieces of fabric in bright colours. Allow to dry and iron flat.

5. Explain that Adinkra cloth is sectioned off into rectangles with a comb dipped in dye. Show them how to cover the stamp with thick paint and print onto the cloth to make a rectangular border. Children may wish to work in pairs and combine a number of different symbols.

6. Leave the cloth to dry and display as a large Adinkra cloth mural.

Masquerade Masks

African masks come in a huge variety of shapes, sizes and styles. Some masks represent powerful wild animals while others are in the form of a human face and are used as representations of spirits of ancestors. It is thought that masks provide a way of communicating with the spirits of ancestors and also a way of controlling the spirits of wild creatures. Masks are worn at masquerades, held to mark important events in the community such as weddings, funerals, other religious ceremonies and the changing of the seasons. The masquerade itself is a male activity with women represented by men in masks. Once a mask is put on, it is believed that the wearer adopts the characteristics of the animal or the person he represents. The masks are made from a variety of materials including wood, leather, metal and cloth.

Resources

- Pictures of African animal masks
- Cartridge paper
- Thin sheets of wood
- Wood shavings, sawdust and chippings
- Natural collage materials such as raffia, wool and feathers
- Scissors
- Paint and brushes

Approach

1 Show the children pictures of African masks including contemporary ones such as the sculpture of a man in a masquerade costume entitled 'Otobo masquerade' (available to download from www. britishmuseum.org; click on 'Research' and type 'Otobo' into the search box).

2 Discuss how some African tribes believe that the animal masks can help them to communicate with and control the spirits of wild creatures. Talk about the type of animals these would include, and research the features of one of these animals.

3 Ask the children to design an animal mask on paper that they will then sculpt in wood.

4 Provide the children with sheets of wood, wood shavings, sawdust, chippings as well as a range of natural collage materials. Encourage the children to explore the different qualities of the wood pieces, looking at texture, colour and shape.

5 Invite the children to use their sketches to create a wooden mask of their chosen animal.

Kente Cloth

Kente cloth is a ceremonial cloth hand-woven by the Asante and other peoples of Ghana. It is made by joining together strips of woven patterns. Each Kente cloth has a different meaning and name depending on the design and the colours used. The Adwinasa pattern is an old design which means 'all motifs used up'. According to legend the weaver wanted to make a unique and beautiful cloth to please the Asantehene, the ruler of the Asante people. He used up all the motifs known to weavers and when he had finished, he said 'adwinasa' (all motifs used up). In the past, Kente cloth was worn by Asante kings and symbolises royalty, wealth and superior craftsmanship.

Resources

- *The Spider Weaver* by Margaret Musgrove and Julia Cairns (Scholastic Inc. 2002) (optional)
- Pictures of Kente cloth
- Strips of paper or felt
- Weaving frames

Approach

1 If possible, read *The Spider Weaver* to the children. The book retells the legend of the origins of Kente cloth, in which two expert weavers called Nana Koragu and Nana Ameyaw come across a spider busily spinning a web.
2 Show the children pictures of Kente cloth and, using strips of paper or felt, invite them to create own Kente strip.
3 Join all the different strips together to create a large Kente collage.
4 Create woven spider patterns in the same way.

Giant Beadwork Necklace

The Maasai people are well known for their beautiful beadwork. The colours, shapes and patterns often carry messages or meanings. The three main colours in their beadwork are red, blue and green. Red represents danger, strength and bravery, blue represents the sky and green the land that grows food for their cattle.

Resources

- Pictures of Maasai beadwork
- Circular pieces of card, cut into segments
- Felt pens
- Beads and sequins
- Glue

Approach

1 Show the children pictures of Maasai beadwork. Discuss the shapes, patterns and colours.
2 Give each child a segment of card and ask them to design a pattern, then colour it in with felt pens.
3 Invite them to decorate the collar with beads and sequins.
4 Display all the designs together in a giant necklace shape.

Cross-curricular Links

- **Art** – Artists Pablo Picasso (1881–1973) and André Dérain (1880–1954) were inspired by African masks. They liked the bold, abstract designs. In the period 1907 to 1909, Picasso painted in a style that was strongly influenced by African art. Find examples of work from this period and discuss the African influences.
- **Literature** – Anansi the Spider is an important figure in Asante folklore. Read some of the stories, such as those in *The Adventures of Spider: West African Folktales* by Joyce Cooper Arkhurst (Little, Brown Books for Young Readers, 1992) and invite the children to write their own.

67

Australian and Oceanic Art

The Aboriginal people are the indigenous natives of Australia and have lived there for more 40,000 years. Aboriginal people believe that all life can be traced back to their ancestor spirits, and that at the beginning of time, the earth was a featureless, desolate place. This was known as *Dreamtime*, the period of time before creation. These ancestor spirits undertook many journeys that criss-crossed Australia in a maze of tracks, known as *dreaming tracks,* often depicted in Australian art as 'maps' painted on bark or canvas. Aboriginal dot painting uses symbols to depict these stories of deep cultural significance.

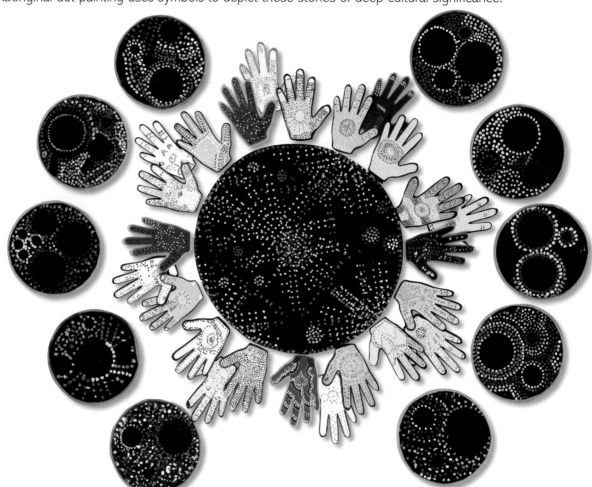

Aboriginal Dot Painting

Resources

- Examples of Dreamtime stories, such as *Stories from the Billabong* by James Vance Marshall (Frances Lincoln, 2008)
- Paper   ● Paint
- Hole-punches
- Silk-screen and squeegee
- Matchsticks and cotton buds

Approach

1 Read some Dreamtime stories to the children.

Explain the background to the creation myths and the history of the Aboriginal people. Show pictures of Aboriginal dot paintings.

2 Demonstrate how dot patterns can be created on a piece of folded paper using a hole-punch. Let the children experiment and when they have a pattern they are happy with place it on the material. Place the silk-screen on top and using the squeegee, pull paint over the screen. Lift off the screen and allow the print to dry.

3 The background of the material can be painted if required.

4 Create more dot patterned pictures using matchsticks and cotton buds dipped in paint.

Bark Paintings

Bark paintings are thought to date back many thousands of years and were originally painted by artists in Arnhem Land, Northern Australia to illustrate Aboriginal stories. They were painted in naturally occurring mineral pigments of red, black, white and yellow on sheets of bark. The pictures often show people and animals on the inside and outside at the same time.

Resources

- Pictures of Aboriginal bark paintings
- Cartridge paper
- Sheets of cork
- Paints and felt pens in 'earthy' colours
- Matchsticks and wood shavings

Approach

1 Look at pictures of Aboriginal bark paintings.
2 Ask the children to sketch out ideas for their own bark paintings on a sheet of paper and then lightly draw the outline of the design in pencil onto a sheet of cork.
3 Use paint and felt pens to colour the picture.
4 Decorate with matchsticks and wood bark or shavings.

Easter Island Moai

Oceanic art is produced by the indigenous island peoples of the south and north-west Pacific, which includes New Zealand, the Solomon Islands and Easter Island. Oceania covers a vast area and the art produced is hugely diverse and individual to each country. Easter Island is a remote and isolated island in the Pacific Ocean and is famous for its stone statues of human figures known as *moai*. Nearly a thousand moai were produced, carved from the island's volcanic rock. The meaning of the *moai* is unclear but they are believed to be representations of deceased ancestors.

Resources

- World map
- Pictures of the moai *Hoa Hakananai'a'* (available to download from www.britishmuseum.org; type '*Hoa Hakananai'a'* into the search box).
- Oasis flower blocks
- Blunt knives or clay tools
- Cartridge paper
- Paint and brushes

Approach

1 Locate Easter Island on a world map. Research the history of the island and its people. Show the children pictures of the moai *Hoa Hakananai'a'*, now in the British Museum. Tell them that it is a huge sculpture – 2.42 metres high and weighing about four tons – and that the name *Hoa Hakananai'a'* means 'stolen or hidden friend'. It was made in around 1000CE. Discuss how these sculptures were made and how they might have been transported to different parts of the island.

2 Give the children blocks of flower arranging oasis blocks, which are easy for young children to sculpt using blunt knives or clay tools.

3 Ask the children to sketch out a moai using the pictures for inspiration and transfer the ideas onto the sculpture.

4 Paint the sculptures in thick poster paint.

Maori Koru Art

The Maori people are the indigenous people of New Zealand and they have a culture rich with stories and legends. The main traditional Maori art forms are weaving and carving. They draw inspiration from their connection with nature. A popular motif in Maori art is the *koru*, a spiral shape based on the curl of a new unfurling silver fern frond. It symbolises new life, growth and strength, and is often used in a repetitive fashion on borders or painted panels called *kowhaiwhai* and painted in red, black and white.

Resources

- Pictures of Maori art showing patterns made with the koru symbol
- The Maori creation story (optional)
- Silk-screen and squeegee
- Red, black and white paints
- Dry fern leaves   ● Cartridge paper

Approach

1 Introduce the children to Maori art and investigate the use of the koru in designs. Explain that it is a symbol and conveys a message. Discuss the message and its relationship to the fern frond.

2 If possible, tell the children the Maori creation story which describes the world being formed by the violent separation of Ranginui, the sky father, and Papatuanuku, the Earth mother.

3 Show the children how to sketch the koru and encourage them to experiment with ideas using the shape, for example, by enlarging it, repeating it, rotating it, curling it and so on.

4 Place a dry fern leaf on top of a sheet of paper. Place the silk-screen on top and, using the squeegee, pull paint over the screen. Lift off the screen and allow the print to dry.

5 Decorate the border with Koru patterns.

Utopian Batiks

Utopian Batiks are contemporary Aboriginal art from the desert region of Utopia approximately 270km north-east of Alice Springs. The batik project was established in the 1970s to provide the Aboriginal women with a source of income. They are very colourful and distinctive batiks mainly in earthen colours of red, yellow, orange and purple. They often relate stories of the Dreamtime, as well as featuring Australian plant and animal motifs.

Resources

- Pictures of Utopian batiks
- Batik cold wax
- Silk material
- Silk paint and brushes
- An iron and kitchen roll

Approach

1 Batik is a resist dyeing process. Explain to the children that wax is painted onto the fabric and that the dye will colour wherever they don't put wax.
2 Show the children pictures of Utopian batiks and discuss the shapes and motifs. Common motifs are spirals, dots, semi-circles and lines.
3 Ask the children to draw a design on a piece of paper and attach a piece of silk on top.
4. Trace over the design with cold batik wax.
5 Allow to dry thoroughly and paint the background with silk paints.
6 Adult help will be needed to iron off the wax between sheets of kitchen roll.
7 Display with some dot pattern designs.

Cross-curricular Links

- **Geography/History** – Australians have a national holiday, Australia Day, on 26 January when they remember their history, culture and achievements. Research the history of the first Europeans to settle in Australia. Put on an Australia Day celebration with Australian food, music and dancing.